THE ECONOMIC
NATURALIST

ROBERT H. FRANK

THE ECONOMIC NATURALIST

In Search of Explanations for Everyday Enigmas

BASIC
BOOKS

A Member of the Perseus Books Group
New York

Books published by Basic Books are available at special discounts for bulk purchases in the United States by corporations, institutions, and other organizations. For more information, please contact the Special Markets Department at the Perseus Books Group, 11 Cambridge Center, Cambridge MA 02142, or call (617) 252-5298 or (800) 255-1514, or e-mail special.markets@perseusbooks.com.

Designed by Jeff Williams

Library of Congress Cataloging-in-Publication Data
Frank, Robert H.
    The economic naturalist : in search of answers to everyday enigmas / Robert H. Frank.
        p.   cm.
    Includes bibliographical references and index.
    ISBN-13: 978-0-465-00217-7 (alk. paper)
    ISBN-10: 0-465-00217-X (alk. paper)
1. Economics.   I. Title.

HB71.F6957 2007
330—dc22

2007001519

For
Thomas C. Schelling

Contents

Acknowledgments

When I first started teaching introductory economics, a senior colleague advised me to begin each class with a joke. It would start students off in a good mood, he explained, and make them more receptive to the ensuing lecture. I never followed his advice. It wasn't that I thought he was wrong in principle. Rather, I thought it would be too hard to come up with a relevant joke each time and felt that telling an irrelevant one would just be pandering.

As luck would have it, however, I stumbled upon a joke that seems just the right vehicle to launch this book. The joke is set in Boston, a city known for its learned cab drivers, many of them dropouts from Harvard and MIT:

> A woman lands at Logan Airport, grabs her luggage, and jumps into a cab, hungry for a good New England seafood dinner. "Take me to a place where I can get scrod," she tells the driver.
>
> Eyebrow arched, the cabbie turns and says, "That's the first time I've heard anyone say that in the pluperfect subjunctive."

Few people actually know what the pluperfect subjunctive tense is. I didn't, or didn't realize I did, so I looked it up on ASK JEEVES:

> The pluperfect subjunctive (or past perfect subjunctive) tense is used to express a hypothetical situation or an action which is contrary to reality. In this case, the verb in the main clause is

conjugated in the conditional form and it is necessary to use the subjunctive in the subordinate clause.

Here's an example that will be familiar to New York Yankees fans from the late 1990s, when Chuck Knoblauch, the team's second baseman, inexplicably lost his ability to complete the short throw to first baseman Tino Martinez: "The Yankees would have been out of the inning if Knoblauch had made the throw to first."

As is clear from the definition and example, the woman in the joke didn't actually use the pluperfect subjective tense at all. If the joke works, it is only because most of us haven't the foggiest idea what this tense is.

Does it matter? Some psychologists once theorized that people couldn't engage in clear counterfactual thinking unless they knew the technical details of the various subjunctive tenses. But this claim doesn't withstand scrutiny. Notice, for instance, that although most American sports announcers don't seem to know the pluperfect subjunctive (or at least choose not to use it), they manage just fine with counterfactual reasoning. Thus, as Yankees announcer Bobby Murcer used to say during those games in the late 1990s, "Knoblauch makes that throw, they're out of the inning."

Knowing about the pluperfect subjunctive is not a bad thing. But if learning to speak a new language is your goal, the time and effort required to learn the explicit technical details of this tense would be far better spent in other ways. Courses that focus most of their energy on such details are no fun for students, and they're also astonishingly ineffective.

I took four years of Spanish in high school and three semesters of German in college. In those courses, we spent a lot of time on the pluperfect subjunctive tense and other grammatical arcana that instructors thought important. But we didn't learn to speak. When I traveled in Spain and Germany, I had great difficulty communicating even basic thoughts in those languages. Many friends have described similar experiences.

My first inkling that there was a more effective way to learn languages came during the instruction I received before serving as a Peace Corps volunteer in Nepal. The program lasted only thirteen weeks and was completely different from my earlier language courses. It never once mentioned the pluperfect subjunctive. Its task was to teach us to speak Nepali, and mastering arcane tenses had no place on the critical path to that goal. The method of instruction was to mimic the way children learn to speak their native language.

Our instructor began with simple sentences and had us repeat them multiple times. The first was, "This hat is expensive." Since shoppers bargain for everything in Nepal, it was a useful sentence. The next step was to announce a different noun—say, socks—and we would have to respond on the fly with the Nepali sentence for, "These socks are expensive." The goal was to get us to respond without thinking about it.

In brief, instructors started with a simple example from a familiar context, had us drill it several times, then had us do slight variations on it, drilling again. Once we could function on our own at the current level—but not before—they would push us a little further.

The program's responsibility was to make sure we were up and running after thirteen weeks. My fellow volunteers and I had to teach science and math in Nepali shortly after arriving in the country. And starting from zero, we did it. The process itself created a sense of empowerment I had never experienced in traditional language courses.

So my first thanks go to my Nepali language instructors of long ago, who opened my eyes to the remarkable effectiveness of the less-is-more approach to learning. As my students and I have discovered during the ensuing decades, this approach can also transform the experience of learning the core ideas of economics.

Students in most introductory economics courses spend much of their time grappling with the economics equivalent of the pluperfect subjunctive tense. In contrast, the economics ideas you will encounter in this book appear only in the context of examples drawn from familiar experiences they help illuminate. Learning economics is like learning to speak a new language. It's important to start slowly and see each idea in multiple contexts. If you discover that this way of learning trumps the one employed in your college introductory course, tip your hat to my Nepali language instructors.

This book is the product of many fine minds. Hal Bierman, Chris Frank, Hayden Frank, Srinagesh Gavirneni, Tom Gilovich, Bob Libby,

Ellen McCollister, Phil Miller, Michael O'Hare, Dennis Regan, and Andy Ruina will recognize the many ways in which their comments on earlier drafts have improved the book. I cannot thank them enough. Others were helpful at further remove. Some readers will recognize the ideas of my former teacher George Akerlof and former colleague Richard Thaler in many of the examples in the book. But my biggest intellectual debt is to Thomas Schelling, the greatest living economic naturalist. I dedicate this book to him.

I'm grateful as well to Andrew Wylie and William Frucht, without whose efforts this book probably would not have ended up in your hands. I also thank Piyush Nayyar, Elizabeth Seward, Maria Cristina Cavagnaro, and Matthew Leighton for invaluable research assistance, and Chrisona Schmidt for superb copyediting.

It was a pleasure to work with Mick Stevens, whose drawings illustrate many of the examples in the book. I am not much given to envy, but if there is a career I can imagine having been more fun than my own, it is his. Over the years, I have tried, whenever possible, to use simple drawings or other illustrations that relate in some way to the examples I discuss in class. For reasons that learning theorists could probably explain, this practice seems to root ideas more firmly in students' minds, even though my drawings are often comically inept and contain no specific economic content. I encourage students to produce their own crude illustrations to accompany the new ideas they encounter. "Doodle on your notes!" I tell them. What a wonderful luxury it was to describe ideas for drawings to one of my favorite New Yorker cartoonists and then have them appear, usually only days later, in much better form than I dared imagine.

I am especially grateful to the John S. Knight Institute for Writing in the Disciplines for enlisting me in its program at Cornell in the early 1980s. Except for my participation in that program, I never would have stumbled upon the economic naturalist writing assignment that led to this book.

But most important, I want to thank my students for the spirited essays that constitute the inspiration for the book. Only a small fraction of the questions they posed made it into the final manuscript. The ones that did are so splendid because of the effort that went into the thousands of essays from which I chose them.

A majority of the questions included in this volume were directly inspired by student essays. Following each, I list the student's name in parentheses. A handful of questions were inspired by articles or books, most of them written by economists, and the relevant author's name also appears in parentheses afer those. Most of the questions with no author credit are based either on examples from my own writings or on examples that I have developed for classes.

There remain three questions, however, that were inspired by student essays that I have been unable to locate. I list these questions here, in the hope that the authors will step forward so that I can credit them properly in subsequent printings: (1) Why is milk sold in rectangular containers, while soft drinks are sold in round ones? p. 18; (2) Why do many bars charge patrons for water but give them peanuts for free? p. 33; and (3) Why do rental car companies impose no penalty for canceling a reservation at the last minute, whereas both hotels and airlines impose significant cancellation charges? p. 91.

In grateful acknowledgment of my former students' contributions, I am donating half my royalties from this volume to Cornell's John S. Knight Institute for Writing in the Disciplines with full confidence that, dollar for dollar, no gift could more enhance the learning experience of future Cornell students.

Introduction

W hy do the keypad buttons on drive-up cash machines have Braille dots? The patrons of these machines are almost always drivers, none of whom are blind. According to my former student Bill Tjoa, ATM producers have to make keypads with Braille dots for their walk-up machines anyway, and so it is cheaper to make all machines the same way. The alternative would be to hold two separate inventories and make sure that each machine went to the right destination. If the Braille dots caused trouble for sighted users, the extra expense might be justified. But they do not.

Braille dots on keypad buttons of drive-up cash machines: Why not?

Mr. Tjoa's question was the title of one of two short papers he submitted in response to the "economic naturalist" writing assignment in my introductory economics course. The specific assignment was "to use a principle, or principles, discussed in the course to pose and answer an interesting question about some pattern of events or behavior that you personally have observed."

"Your space limit," I wrote, "is 500 words. Many excellent papers are significantly shorter than that. Please do not lard your essay with complex terminology. Imagine yourself talking to a relative who has never had a course in economics. The best papers are ones that would be clearly intelligible to such a person, and typically these papers do not use any algebra or graphs."

Like Bill Tjoa's question about ATM keypads, the best ones entail an element of paradox. For example, my all-time favorite was submitted in 1997 by Jennifer Dulski, who asked, "Why do brides spend so much money—often many thousands of dollars—on wedding dresses they will never wear again, while grooms often rent cheap tuxedos, even though they will have many future occasions that call for one?"

Dulski argued that because most brides wish to make a fashion statement on their wedding day, a rental company would have to carry a huge stock of distinctive gowns—perhaps forty or fifty in each size. Each garment would thus be rented only infrequently, perhaps just once every four or five years. The company would have to charge a rental fee greater than the purchase price of the garment just to cover its costs. And since buying would be cheaper, no one would rent. In contrast, because grooms are willing to settle for a standard style, a rental company can serve this market with an inventory of only two or three tuxedos in each size. So each suit gets rented several times a year, enabling a rental fee that is only a fraction of its purchase price.

This book is a collection of the most interesting economic naturalist examples I have collected over the years. It is intended for people who, like Bill Tjoa and Jennifer Dulski, take pleasure in unraveling the mysteries of everyday human behavior. Although many consider economics an arcane and incomprehensible subject, its basic principles are simple and commonsensical. Seeing these principles at work in the context of concrete examples provides an opportunity to master them without effort.

Unfortunately that is not how economics is usually taught in college courses. Shortly after I began teaching at Cornell University, several friends living in different cities mailed me copies of this Ed Arno cartoon:

Drawing by Ed Arno. © 1974 The New Yorker Magazine, Inc.

"I'd like to introduce you to Marty Thorndecker.
He's an economist, but he's really very nice."

Cartoons are data. If people find them funny, that tells us something about the world. Even before Arno's cartoon appeared, I had begun to notice that when people I met at social gatherings asked me what I did for a living, they seemed disappointed when I told them I was an economist. I began asking why. On reflection, many would mention having taken an introductory economics course years before that had "all those horrible graphs."

Nineteen percent of American undergraduates take only one economics course, another 21 percent take more than one, and only 2 percent go on to major in economics. A negligible fraction pursues Ph.D. work in economics. Yet many introductory economics courses, abrim with equations and graphs, are addressed to that negligible fraction.

The result is that most students in these courses don't learn much. When students are given tests designed to probe their knowledge of basic economics six months after taking the course, they do not perform significantly better than others who never took an introductory course. This is scandalous. How can a university justify charging thousands of dollars for courses that add no value?

Even the most basic principles of economics don't seem to be getting across. If you ever took an economics course, you at least heard the term "opportunity cost." The opportunity cost of engaging in an activity is the value of everything you must give up to pursue it.

To illustrate, suppose you won a free ticket to see an Eric Clapton concert tonight. You can't resell it. Bob Dylan is performing on the same night and his concert is the only other activity you are considering. A Dylan ticket costs $40 and on any given day you would be willing to pay as much as $50 to see him perform. (In other words, if Dylan tickets sold for more than $50, you would pass on the opportunity to see him even if you had nothing else to do.) There is no other cost of seeing either performer. What is your opportunity cost of attending the Clapton concert?

The only thing of value you must sacrifice to attend the Clapton concert is seeing the Dylan concert. By not attending the Dylan concert, you miss out on a performance that would have been worth $50 to you, but you also avoid having to spend $40 for the Dylan ticket. So the value of what you give up by not seeing him is $50 − $40 = $10. If seeing Clapton is worth at least $10 to you, you should attend his concert. Otherwise you should see Dylan.

Opportunity cost is, by consensus, one of the two or three most important ideas in introductory economics. Yet we now have persuasive evidence that most students do not master this concept in any fundamental way. The economists Paul Ferraro and Laura Taylor recently posed the Clapton/Dylan question to groups of students to see whether they could answer it. They gave their respondents only four choices:

a. $0

b. $10

c. $40

d. $50

As noted, the correct answer is $10, the value of what you sacrifice by not attending the Dylan concert. Yet when Ferraro and Taylor posed this question to 270 undergraduates who had previously taken a course in economics, only 7.4 percent of them answered it correctly. Since there were only four choices, students who picked at random would have had a correct response rate of 25 percent. A little bit of knowledge seems to be a dangerous thing here.

When Ferraro and Taylor posed the same question to eighty-eight students who had never taken an economics course, 17.2 percent answered it correctly—more than twice the correct response rate as for former economics students, but still less than chance.

Why didn't the economics students perform better? The main reason, I suspect, is that opportunity cost is only one of several hundred concepts that professors throw at students during the typical introductory course, and it simply goes by in a blur. If students don't spend enough time on it and use it repeatedly in different examples, it never really sinks in.

But Ferraro and Taylor suggest another possibility: the instructors who teach economics may not have mastered the basic opportunity cost concept themselves. When the researchers posed the same question to a sample of 199 professional economists at the annual American Economic Association meetings in 2005, only 21.6 percent chose the correct answer; 25.1 percent thought the opportunity cost of attending the Clapton concert was $0, 25.6 percent thought it was $40, and 27.6 percent thought it was $50.

When Ferraro and Taylor examined the leading introductory economics textbooks, they discovered that most did not devote sufficient attention to the opportunity cost concept to enable students to answer the Dylan/Clapton question. They also noted that the concept does not receive patient, in-depth treatment in textbooks beyond the introductory level and that the term "opportunity cost" does not even appear in the indexes of leading graduate microeconomics texts.

Yet opportunity cost helps explain a host of interesting behavior patterns. Consider, for example, the widely remarked cultural differences between large coastal cities in the United States and smaller cities in the

Midwest. Why do residents of Manhattan tend to be rude and impatient, but residents of Topeka friendly and courteous?

You could argue with the premise, of course, but most people seem to find it roughly descriptive. If you ask for directions in Topeka, people stop and help you; in Manhattan, they may not even make eye contact. Because Manhattan has the highest wage rate and the richest menu of things to do of any city on the planet, the opportunity cost of people's time is very high there. So perhaps it is only to be expected that New Yorkers would be a little quicker to show impatience.

I call my students' writing assignment the "economic naturalist" because it was inspired by the kinds of questions that an introductory course in biology enables students to answer. If you know a little evolutionary theory, you can see things you didn't notice before. The theory identifies texture and pattern in the world that is stimulating to recognize and think about.

For example, here is a standard Darwinian question: Why are males bigger than females in most vertebrate species? Bull elephant seals, for instance, can exceed twenty feet in length and weigh six thousand pounds—as much as a Lincoln Navigator—whereas female elephant seals weigh only eight hundred to twelve hundred pounds.

Photo by Stan Russell.

Why is the bull elephant seal so much bigger than the cow?

Similar sexual dimorphism is observed in most vertebrate species. The Darwinian explanation is that most vertebrates are polygynous (meaning that males take more than one mate if they can), and so males must compete for access to females. Bull elephant seals pummel one another on the beach for hours at a time until one finally retreats, bloodied and exhausted.

The winners of these battles command nearly exclusive sexual access to harems of as many as one hundred females. This is a Darwinian prize of the first order, and it explains why males are so much bigger. A male with a mutant gene for larger size would be more likely to prevail in fights with other males, which means that this gene would appear with higher frequency in the next generation. In short, the reason males are so large is that small males seldom gain access to females.

A similar explanation accounts for the large tail displays in peacocks. Experiments have demonstrated that peahens prefer peacocks with longer tail feathers, which are thought to be a signal of robust health, since parasite-ridden males cannot maintain a bright, long tail.

For both the large bull elephant seal and the peacock with a long tail display, what is advantageous to males individually is disadvantageous to them as a group. A six-thousand-pound seal, for example, finds it harder to escape from the great white shark, its principal predator. If all bulls could cut their weight by half, each would be better off. The outcome of each fight would be the same as before, yet all would be better able to escape from predators. Similarly, if all peacocks' tail displays were reduced by half, females would still choose the same males as before, yet all peacocks would be better able to escape from predators. But bull elephant seals are stuck with their massive size and peacocks are stuck with their long tail feathers.

Of course evolutionary arms races do not continue indefinitely. At some point, the added vulnerability inherent in larger size or longer tail displays begins to outweigh the benefit of increased access to females. That balance of costs and benefits is reflected in the characteristics of surviving males.

The biologist's narrative is interesting. It coheres. And it seems to be right. Thus if you look at monogamous species, ones in which males and females pair off for life, you don't see sexual dimorphism. This is

Photo by David Levine.

*The exception that proves the rule: In the monogamous albatross,
males and females are about the same size.*

"the exception that proves the rule" in the old-fashioned sense of the
verb "to prove": it tests the rule. Polygyny led to the prediction that
males would be bigger. And in its absence males aren't bigger. For example, because the albatross is monogamous, theory predicts that males
and females will be roughly the same size, which in fact they are.

The biologist's narrative regarding sexual dimorphism has legs. It is
easy to remember and satisfying to recount to others. If you can tell such
stories and understand why they make sense, you have a far better grasp
of biology than if you've simply memorized that birds belong to Class
Aves. It is the same with narrative explanations based on principles of
economics.

Most introductory economics courses (and my own was no exception in the early days) make little use of narrative. Instead, they inun-
date students with equations and graphs. Mathematical formalism has
been an enormously important source of intellectual progress in economics, but it has not proved an effective vehicle for introducing new-

comers to our subject. Except for engineering students and a handful of others with extensive prior training in math, most students who attempt to learn economics primarily through equations and graphs never really grasp that distinctive mind-set known as "thinking like an economist." Most of them spend so much effort trying to make sense of the mathematical details that the intuition behind economic ideas escapes them.

The human brain is remarkably flexible, an organ with the capacity to absorb new information in myriad different forms. But information gets into most brains more easily in some forms than others. In most cases, students process equations and graphs only with difficulty. But because our species evolved as storytellers, virtually everyone finds it easy to absorb the corresponding information in narrative form.

I stumbled onto this insight by chance some twenty years ago when I participated in the writing across the disciplines program at Cornell, which was inspired by research showing that one of the best ways to learn about something is to write about it. As Walter Doyle and Kathy Carter, two proponents of the narrative theory of learning, have written, "At its core, the narrative perspective holds that human beings have a universal predisposition to 'story' their experience, that is, to impose a narrative interpretation on information and experience." Psychologist Jerome Bruner, another narrative learning theorist, observes that children "turn things into stories, and when they try to make sense of their life they use the storied version of their experience as the basis for further reflection. . . . If they don't catch something in a narrative structure, it doesn't get remembered very well, and it doesn't seem to be accessible for further kinds of mulling over."

In short, the human brain's specialty seems to be absorbing information in narrative form. My economic naturalist writing assignment plays directly to this strength. It calls for the title of each student's paper to be a question. For three reasons, I have found it useful to insist that students pose the most interesting questions they can. First, to come up with an interesting question, they must usually consider numerous preliminary questions, and this itself is a useful exercise. Second, students who come up with interesting questions have more fun with the assignment and devote more energy to it. And third, the student who poses an interesting question is more likely to tell others about it. If you can't actually take an idea outside the classroom and use it, you don't really get it. But once you use it on your own, it is yours forever.

The Cost-Benefit Principle

The mother of all economic ideas is the cost-benefit principle. It says you should take an action if and only if the extra benefit from taking it is greater than the extra cost. How simple could a principle be? Still, it is not always easy to apply.

> *Example 1.* You are about to buy a $20 alarm clock at the campus store next door when a friend tells you that the same clock is available for $10 at the Kmart downtown. Do you go downtown and get the clock for $10? Or do you buy it at the nearby campus store? In either case, if the clock malfunctions under warranty, you must send it to the manufacturer for repairs.

Of course, there is no universally right or wrong answer. Each person has to weigh the relevant costs and benefits. But when we ask people what they would do in this situation, most say they would buy the clock at Kmart.

Now consider this question:

> *Example 2.* You are about to buy a laptop for $2,510 at the campus store next door. You can get the very same laptop downtown at Kmart for $2,500 (and it comes with the same guarantee: no matter where you buy it, you have to send it to the manufacturer for repairs if it breaks). Where would you buy the laptop?

This time, most people say they would buy it at the campus store. By itself, that isn't a wrong answer. But if we ask what a rational person *should* do in these two cases, the cost-benefit principle makes clear that both answers must be the same. After all, the benefit of going downtown is $10 in each case, the dollar amount you save. The cost is whatever value you assign to the hassle of going downtown. That is also the same in the two cases. And if the cost is the same and the benefit is the same in both cases, then the answer should be the same as well.

Most people seem to think, however, that saving 50 percent by buying the clock downtown is somehow a bigger benefit than saving only $10 on the $2,510 laptop. But that is not the right way to think about it. Thinking in percentage terms works reasonably well in other contexts, but not here.

So weighing costs and benefits is obviously what you should do. Seeing how the cost-benefit principle works in the context of a surprising example gives you an interesting story to tell. Pose these questions to friends and see how they do. Having these conversations will deepen your mastery of the cost-benefit principle.

Immediately after I show students examples that illustrate a general principle, I give them an exercise that requires them to employ the principle on their own. Here's the question I pose to them after they've seen the clock and computer examples:

> *Example 3.* You have two business trips coming up and a discount coupon you can use on only one of them. You can save either $90 on your $200 trip to Chicago or $100 on your $2,000 trip to Tokyo. For which trip should you use your coupon?

Almost everybody answers correctly that you should use it for the Tokyo trip because you will save $100, which is better than saving $90. But the fact that everyone gets it right doesn't mean that the question wasn't worth asking. Again, if your goal is for the core ideas to become part of your working knowledge, the only way that can happen is through engagement and repetition.

I chose the questions in this volume not just because I found them interesting but because they actively engage the most important principles of basic economics. My hope is that you will find this book an effortless, even entertaining, way to learn these principles. And because the questions are interesting and the answers brief, they provide good fodder for conversation.

I tell my students that their answers to the questions should be viewed as intelligent hypotheses suitable for further refinement and testing. They are not meant to be the final word. When Ben Bernanke and I described Bill Tjoa's example about drive-up ATM keypads with Braille dots in our introductory economics textbook, somebody sent me an angry e-mail saying that the real reason for the dots is that the Americans with Disabilities Act requires them. He sent me a link to a web page documenting his claim. Sure enough, there is a requirement that all ATM keypads have Braille dots, even at drive-up locations. Having Braille dots on drive-up machines might even be useful on rare occasions, as when a blind person visits a drive-up machine in a taxi and does not want to reveal his PIN to the driver.

I wrote back to my correspondent that I tell my students their answers don't have to be correct. But I also urged him to think about the circumstances under which the regulation was adopted. If it had been significantly more costly to require Braille dots on the drive-up machines, would the rule have been enacted? Almost certainly not. The fact is that adding them was costless. And since the dots cause no harm and might occasionally be of use, regulators might well find it advantageous to require them, thereby enabling themselves to say, at year's end, that they had done something useful. In this case, Mr. Tjoa's explanation makes better sense than my angry correspondent's. But in other cases there are bound to be better or more complete answers out there.

So read the answers to the questions with a critical eye. You may have personal knowledge that enables you to improve them. I was told by the proprietor of a wedding gown boutique, for example, that another reason brides buy their dresses rather than rent them is that wedding gowns tend to be form fitting in the torso and often require extensive alterations that could not be performed repeatedly on rental garments. It's a fair point, but it doesn't nullify the core economic insight in Jennifer Dulski's explanation.

1

Rectangular Milk Cartons and Cylindrical Soda Cans

The Economics of Product Design

Why do products take their particular forms? No intelligent answer to this question could be complete without at least an implicit invocation of the cost-benefit principle. For example, Bill Tjoa's explanation for Braille dots on the keypad buttons of drive-up cash machines rests on this principle. Producers kept dots on the drive-up machines because the cost of producing two different types of machines was greater than any reasonable estimate of the corresponding benefit.

In general, producers have no incentive to add a product feature unless it enhances the product's value (in other words, its benefit) to consumers by more than enough to cover its cost. In almost every instance, product design entails a trade-off between features that would be most pleasing to consumers and each seller's need to keep prices low enough to remain competitive.

This trade-off is nicely illustrated in the evolution of automobile features. I bought my first car in the spring of 1961, when I was a high school junior. The classified ad that led me to it read something like this: "1955 Pontiac Chieftain two-door, V8, radio, heater, stick shift, $375 or best offer." Today, of course, all cars have heaters, but in 1955 they were optional. Many cars sold in South Florida, where I lived, did not have them. Even there, however, a heater would have been nice on at least a few days each winter. But incomes were much lower then, and many buyers were willing to forgo that luxury to get a slight break on price. At that time, a manufacturer that offered only cars with heaters would have risked losing business to rivals that offered cheaper models without them.

As incomes rose, however, the number of consumers willing to endure winter's chill to save a few dollars steadily diminished. Once the demand for cars without heaters fell below a certain point, dealers no longer wanted to keep them in showrooms. They would have been able to supply them as higher-priced, custom orders, but clearly no one would pay extra for the option of doing without a heater. Eventually cars without heaters disappeared.

My Pontiac's V8 engine was a common choice of car buyers in 1955, when the only other widely available option was a six-cylinder engine. The benefit of the V8 was that it provided noticeably better acceleration than the six. Its cost, in addition to its higher purchase price, was that it consumed a little more fuel. But gasoline was still cheap in those days.

Then came the Arab oil embargoes of the 1970s. Gasoline that had sold for thirty-eight cents a gallon in mid-1973 jumped to fifty-two cents a gallon later that year. A second supply interruption in 1979 drove the price to $1.19 by 1980. In the wake of these increases, many consumers decided that the V8's superior acceleration no longer met the cost-benefit test, and these engines all but disappeared. Six-cylinder engines were still common, but the four-cylinder engine, which was rarely offered in American cars before the 1970s, quickly became the engine of choice.

By the early 1980s, however, gasoline prices had stabilized in absolute terms and actually began falling relative to the prices of other goods. By 1999, the price of a gallon of gasoline stood at $1.40 a gallon, which was lower in real terms than the $0.38 a gallon price of mid-1973 (meaning that $1.40 in 1999 would buy fewer other goods and services than thirty-eight cents would have bought in 1973). So it is hardly surprising that engine sizes began increasing again in the 1990s.

As gasoline prices have again escalated in recent years, we are seeing a rerun of the trends of the 1970s. Even before the price reached $3 a gallon in 2005, for instance, the Ford Motor Company had discontinued production of its largest SUV, the 10-miles-per-gallon, 7,500-pound Excursion. Fuel-efficient hybrids are now in such demand that dealers often sell them for more than their sticker prices.

The pattern, in short, is that product design features are dictated by the cost-benefit principle. Again, this principle says that an action should be taken if, and only if, its benefit is at least as great as its cost. Thus a product design feature should not be added unless its benefit (as measured by the amount consumers are willing to pay extra for it) is at least as large as its cost (as measured by the extra expense that producers incur by adding it).

This principle is also visible in the evolution of transmissions. The manual transmission on my 1955 Pontiac had only three forward speeds, which was then the norm. The manual transmission on the car I drive today has six forward speeds. Manufacturers could easily have built transmissions with six forward speeds in 1955. Why didn't they?

Here, too, producers have to weigh the cost of product enhancements against consumers' willingness to pay for them. On the cost side, since each forward speed adds to the cost of producing a transmission, the price of a car must be higher the more forward speeds it has. Will consumers be willing to pay the higher price? On the benefit side, adding forward speeds improves both acceleration and fuel economy. So the answer will depend on how much consumers are willing to pay for these advantages.

Unless its transmission had at least two, or even three, forward speeds, a car would scarcely be functional. (If there were only one, which would you choose? First gear? Second?) So on the product-design scale, my 1955 Pontiac's three-speed transmission was clearly at the minimalist end. Because we are more prosperous now than in 1955, we are willing to pay more for enhanced acceleration. Additional forward speeds have also become more attractive because the gasoline they save is more expensive than it used to be. Together, these changes explain the disappearance of manual transmissions with three forward speeds.

As the examples discussed in this chapter will make clear, the same cost-benefit principle that governs the evolution of automobile design also applies to virtually every product and service. The first three examples illustrate the idea that a product feature is less likely to be added if instances in which it would be useful are relatively infrequent.

Why does a light come on when you open the refrigerator but not when you open the freezer? (Karim Abdallah)

The economic naturalist's impulse in searching for an answer to this question is to examine the relevant costs and benefits. In both compartments of the appliance, the cost of installing a light that comes on automatically when you open the door is essentially the same. It is also what economists call a fixed cost, which in this context means it does not vary with the number of times you open the door. On the benefit side, having a light inside either compartment makes it easier to find things. Since most people open the refrigerator far more often than the freezer, the benefit of having a light in the refrigerator is considerably larger. So with the cost of adding a light the same in both cases, the cost-benefit test for whether to add a light is more likely to be satisfied for the refrigerator than for the freezer.

Of course, not all consumers place the same value on the convenience afforded by a light in the freezer. In general, the benefit of such features, as measured by what people are willing to pay for them, tends to increase as income increases. The cost-benefit principle thus predicts that consumers with extremely high incomes might find the convenience of having a light in the freezer well worth the extra cost. And indeed, the Sub-Zero Pro 48 refrigerator has a light not only in its freezer but also in its separate ice drawer. The price of this unit? $14,450. The Sub-Zero Pro 48 is thus another example of the exception that proves the rule.

Why can laptop computers, but not most other appliances, operate on any country's electrical standard? *(Minsoo Bae)*

Although electrical systems in the United States deliver current to homes mostly at 110 volts, in many other countries the standard is 220 volts. The power cords on laptop computers have an internal transformer, which means that laptops can operate on either voltage standard. In contrast, televisions and refrigerators can operate only on whichever standard they were manufactured for. To use an American refrigerator in France, one must buy a separate transformer to convert the French power source from 220 volts to 110 volts. Similarly, to operate a Korean television in the United States, one must buy a separate transformer to convert the American power source from 110 to 220 volts. Why aren't all electrical appliances as versatile as laptops?

Delivering power at 220 rather than 110 volts is a little cheaper but slightly more dangerous. There was considerable debate in most countries about which system to adopt, but once a decision was made, it entailed a massive commitment of capital to the system chosen. It is thus unrealistic to expect that countries will move to a uniform voltage standard in the near future. So people who travel from country to country with their appliances will need some means of ensuring that they can operate them on different voltage standards.

Adding an internal transformer to any appliance would enable it to meet this demand, but doing so would also increase its cost. Given that the overwhelming majority of refrigerators, washing machines, televisions, and other appliances sold in any country never leave that country, it makes little sense to bear the additional expense of adding internal transformers.

Laptop computers were a conspicuous exception, especially in the early days of production. Early adopters were disproportionately people who took their machines with them when they traveled on both domestic and international business trips. For these people, having to carry a bulky transformer on international flights would have been an unacceptable burden. And so laptop computer makers included internal transformers with their products from the beginning.

Why do twenty-four-hour convenience stores have locks on their doors?
(Leanna Beck, Ebony Johnson)

Many convenience stores are open 24 hours a day, 365 days a year. Since they never lock their doors, why do they bother to install doors with locks on them?

It is always possible, of course, that an emergency could force such a store to close at least briefly. In the wake of Hurricane Katrina, for example, residents of New Orleans were forced to evacuate with little notice. And needless to say, an unlocked store with no employees on site becomes a sitting duck for looters.

But even if the possibility of closing could be ruled out with certainty, it is doubtful that a store would find it advantageous to purchase doors without locks.

The vast majority of industrial doors are sold to establishments that are not open twenty-four hours a day. These establishments have obvious reasons for wanting locks on their doors. So, given that most industrial doors are sold with locks, it is probably cheaper to make all doors the same way, just as it is cheaper to put Braille dots on all ATM keypads, even those destined for drive-up machines.

SOMETIMES, as the next two examples suggest, the details of product design appear to be dictated in part by the laws of geometry.

Why is milk sold in rectangular containers, while soft drinks are sold in round ones?

Virtually all soft drink containers, whether aluminum or glass, are cylindrical. Milk containers are almost always rectangular in cross-section. Rectangular containers use shelf space more economically than cylindrical ones. So why do soft drink producers stick with cylindrical containers?

One possibility is that because soft drinks are often consumed directly from the container, the extra cost of storing cylindrical containers is justified because they fit more comfortably in the hand. This is less of

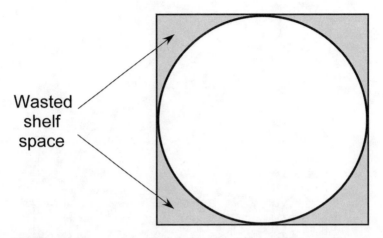

Wasted
shelf
space

If milk containers were cylindrical, we would need larger refrigerators.

an issue in the case of milk, which is typically not consumed directly from the container.

But even if most people drank milk straight from the carton, the cost-benefit principle suggests that it would be unlikely to be sold in cylindrical containers. Although rectangular containers economize on shelf space, irrespective of their contents, the shelf space they save is more valuable in the case of milk than in the case of soft drinks. Most soft drinks in supermarkets are stored on open shelves, which are cheap to buy and have no operating costs. Milk is exclusively stored in refrigerated cabinets, which are both expensive to purchase and costly to operate. Shelf space inside these cabinets thus comes at a premium, and hence the added benefit of packaging milk in rectangular containers.

Why are aluminum soda cans more expensive to produce than necessary?
(Charles Redding)

The task of a soda can is to contain the beverage within it. The twelve-ounce aluminum soft drink containers sold in most parts of the world are cylinders almost twice as tall (height = 12 centimeters) as they are wide (diameter = 6.5 centimeters). Making these cans shorter and wider would require substantially less aluminum. For example, a

Standard soft drink cans would require less aluminum
if they were shorter and wider.

cylindrical can with a height of 7.8 centimeters and a diameter of 7.6 centimeters would require approximately 30 percent less aluminum than the standard can yet would hold the same volume. Since the shorter cans would be cheaper to produce, why are soft drinks still sold in the taller ones?

One possible answer is that consumers are fooled by the vertical illusion—an optical illusion well-known to psychologists. When asked which of the two bars shown in the figure on the following page is longer, for example, most people answer confidently that it is the vertical one. Yet as you can easily verify, the two bars are exactly the same length.

Consumers might thus be reluctant to purchase soft drinks sold in shorter cans, believing they contain less soda. This explanation, however, would appear to imply that rival sellers were passing up easy profit opportunities. That is, if an optical illusion were the only thing preventing consumers from choosing shorter cans, rival sellers could offer soda in such cans, pointing out in plain language that their containers hold exactly the same amount as traditional cans. And since the shorter cans are cheaper to produce, sellers who sold soft drinks in them could offer slightly lower prices than traditional producers and still cover all their

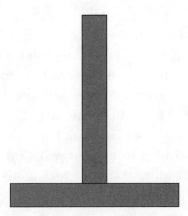

The vertical illusion: Although the vertical bar seems longer, it isn't.

costs. So if an optical illusion were the only problem, there would be easy profit opportunities available to rival sellers.

Another possibility is that soft drink buyers prefer the looks of the taller can. Even if they knew it contained exactly the same amount of soda as the shorter version, they might thus be willing to pay a small premium for it, just as they are willing to pay more for a hotel room with a nice view.

PRODUCT DESIGN FEATURES sometimes reflect sophisticated considerations of how different features would affect user behavior. Someone who wants to avoid speeding tickets, for example, might be willing to pay extra for an automobile equipped to sound a warning when its driver exceeds the posted speed limit. The next two examples illustrate products that reflect strategic decisions on the part of manufacturers about how specific design features will affect product use.

Why are newspapers, but not soft drinks, sold in vending machines that allow customers to take more units than they pay for? *(Brendan Quigley)*

If you put four quarters into a soft drink vending machine and push the Coke button, a cold, twelve-ounce can of Coke will tumble down the chute. If you want a second one, you'll need to deposit four more quarters. In contrast, if you put four quarters into a newspaper vending machine, the front door of the machine opens, providing easy access to the entire stack of today's edition of the *New York Times.* You're entitled to take only one, of course, and most customers observe that limit. But why are newspaper machines built to such low security standards?

The obvious advantage is that such machines are much less costly to build. There is no need for complex mechanical devices to feed a single newspaper out through a slot. The coins trip a simple lever that releases the latch on the machine's front door, which resets once the door is closed. Soft drink vending machines would also be cheaper if constructed in a similar way. So the rationale for the difference in design must reside on the benefit side.

The key distinction between the two products is that whereas a dishonest consumer would benefit from taking more soft drinks than he paid for, he would have little reason for taking more than one newspaper. Having ten copies would make him no better off than having only one.

Why are the fuel filler doors on the driver's side of some cars but on the passenger's side of others? *(Patty Yu)*

One of the most frustrating experiences of driving a rental car is to pull up at a gas pump as you would when driving your own car, only to discover that the gas tank is located on the side of the car away from the pump. Auto manufacturers could eliminate this difficulty simply by putting fuel filler doors always on the same side of the car. Why don't they?

In the United States and other countries in which motorists drive on the right side of the road, it is easier to turn right than to turn left across oncoming traffic. A majority of drivers will thus buy gas at stations they can enter by turning right. Suppose gas tanks were always on the driver's side of the car. Drivers would then have to park on the right side of an open pump in order to fill their tanks. During crowded hours, all spots on the right sides of pumps would be filled even while most spots on the left sides of pumps remained empty.

Putting the fuel filler doors on different sides of different cars thus means that some cars can access pumps from the left. And this makes it less likely that drivers will have to wait in line for gas. That benefit

Drawing by Mick Stevens.

Gas lines would be longer if fuel-filler doors were always on the driver's side.

greatly outweighs the cost of occasionally pulling up to the wrong side of the pump in a rental car.

In some cases product design is dictated not only by how the product is likely to be used but also by the fact that the product aims to communicate information to the user. And as the next two examples illustrate, information is easier to absorb or cheaper to produce in some forms than in others.

Why are almost all cabs in Manhattan yellow sedans, while most cabs in Ithaca are minivans in a variety of colors? *(Andrei Tchernoivanov)*

Gaze down onto 34th Street from atop the Empire State Building in Manhattan and you may think that 70 percent of all vehicles on the road are bright yellow sedans. Apart from an occasional Lotus or Lamborghini, virtually all of these yellow vehicles are taxis, most of them Ford Crown Victoria sedans. In Ithaca, a small university town in upstate New York, none of the taxis are yellow and almost all of them are minivans. Why this difference?

Although it is possible to summon a cab by phone in Manhattan, it is far more common to hail one as it cruises by. It is therefore advantageous for taxis to be as visible as possible. Research has shown that bright yellow is the best color for this purpose. (Red was once thought the most visible color, which is why fire engines used to be painted red. But many fire departments have now begun painting their engines yellow.)

In Manhattan, the typical occupied taxi carries only a single passenger, and a cab driver would rarely benefit by being able to carry more than four. New York cab drivers are thus more likely to find sedans attractive because they are cheaper than minivans and can easily accommodate most demands.

The pattern of taxi demand is different in Ithaca. Owning a car is much cheaper there than in Manhattan, where parking alone can cost more than $500 a month, so most people own one. Since there are relatively few Ithacans who rely on taxis, it is uneconomical for taxis to cruise the streets. Instead, people summon one by phone. Taxi drivers in Ithaca thus see little advantage in painting their vehicles yellow.

Someone might object that taxis in New York are yellow because city regulators require all cruising cabs to be that color. It's true, but this objection resembles my angry correspondent's objection that Braille dots are on the keypads of drive-up cash machines because regulations require them. When taxi regulators adopted the color rule in the wake of industry scandals, their goal was to provide an easy means for passengers to identify legally licensed, regulated taxis. They chose yellow because that was the predominant color of taxis at the time. The hypothesis that cabs are yellow because of the color's high visibility provides a plausible account of why most cabs were yellow before the regulation was adopted.

Ithaca cab drivers favor minivans over sedans because passengers there commonly travel in groups. Students and others who don't own cars in Ithaca tend to have low incomes and thus find it attractive to economize by sharing taxis. For example, while the typical LaGuardia airport taxi ferries only a single passenger into the city, the typical Ithaca airport taxi carries a group of six or more.

Why are the portraits on coins done in profile while those on paper money are in full face? *(Andrew Lack)*

Examine the change in your pocket and you'll notice that the faces of past presidents that appear on the penny (Lincoln), nickel (Jefferson), dime (Roosevelt), quarter (Washington), and half-dollar (Kennedy) are all in profile. But look through the paper money in your wallet and you'll see no profiles. On the bills, artists' portraits of Presidents Washington ($1), Lincoln ($5), Hamilton ($10), Jackson ($20), Grant ($50), and Franklin ($100) are all rendered in full-face form. With occasional exceptions, the same pattern holds for other countries: profiles on coins and full-face portraits on paper bills. Why this difference?

The short answer is that although artists generally prefer full-face portraits, the technical difficulties of engraving metals make it more difficult to create a recognizable full-face portrait on coins. The relief available for portraits on coins is typically less than sixteen-hundredths of an inch, which makes it difficult to achieve the detail generally necessary for an easily recognizable full-face portrait. In contrast, when a face is portrayed in profile, the subject is often easy to recognize from the silhouette alone. The details necessary for recognizable full-face portraits could be engraved on coins, but only at considerable expense. And much of the fine detail would wear off quickly as the coins circulated.

If profiles are easier to produce and recognize, why not put them on bills as well? On paper money, the added complexity of full-face portraits may help foil counterfeiters.

THE FINAL TWO EXAMPLES in this chapter illustrate that product design features sometimes cannot be understood unless we take explicit account of historical commitments.

Why are DVDs sold in much larger packages than CDs, even though the two types of disc are exactly the same size? *(Laura Enos)*

CDs come in cases that are 148 millimeters wide and 125 millimeters high. In contrast, DVDs are sold in cases that are 104.5 millimeters wide and 191 millimeters high. Why use such different packaging for discs of identical size?

A little digging reveals the historical origins of this difference. Prior to the appearance of digital CDs, most music was sold on vinyl discs, which were packaged in close-fitting sleeves that measured 302 millimeters square. The racks on which vinyl discs were displayed were just wide enough, in other words, to accommodate two rows of CD cases with a divider between them. Making the CD cases a little less than half as wide as the album sleeves they were replacing thus enabled retailers to avoid the substantial costs of replacing their storage and display racks.

Similar considerations seem to have driven the decision regarding DVD packaging. Before DVDs became popular, most film rental stores carried videotapes in the VHS format, which were packaged in form-fitting boxes that measured 135 millimeters wide and 191 millimeters high. These videos were typically displayed side by side with their spines out. Making DVD cases the same height enabled stores to display their new DVD stocks on existing shelves while consumers were in the process of switching over to the new format. Making the DVD package the same height as the VHS package also made switching to DVDs more attractive for consumers, since they could store their new DVDs on the same shelves they used for their VHS tapes.

Why do women's clothes always button from the left, while men's clothes always button from the right? *(Gordon Wilde, Katie Willers, and others)*

It is hardly surprising that clothing manufacturers might adhere to uniform standards for the various features of garments bought by any given group. What seems strange, however, is that the standard adopted for women is precisely the opposite of the one for men. If the standard were completely arbitrary, that would be one thing. But the men's standard would appear to make more sense for women as well. After all, approxi-

In matters of dress, history matters.

mately 90 percent of the world's population—male and female—is right-handed, and it is somewhat easier for right-handers to button shirts from the right. So why do women's garments button from the left?

This is an example in which history *really* seems to matter. When buttons first appeared in the seventeenth century, they were seen only on garments of the wealthy. At that time it was the custom for men to dress themselves and for women to be dressed by servants. Having women's shirts button from the left thus made things easier for the mostly right-handed servants who dressed them. Having men's shirts button from the right made sense not just because most men dressed themselves, but also because a sword drawn from the left hip with the right hand would be less likely to become caught in the shirt.

Today virtually no women are dressed by servants, so why is button-ing from the left still the norm for women? A norm, once established, resists change. At a time when all women's shirts buttoned from the left, it would have been risky for any single manufacturer to offer women's shirts that buttoned from the right. After all, women had grown accustomed to shirts that buttoned from the left and would have to develop new habits and skills to switch. Beyond that practical difficulty, some women might also have found it socially awkward to appear in public wearing shirts that buttoned from the right, since anyone who noticed would assume they were wearing men's shirts.

2

Free Peanuts and Expensive Batteries

Supply and Demand in Action

T he story is told of two economists on their way to lunch when they spot what appears to be a $100 bill lying on the sidewalk. When the younger economist stoops to pick it up, his older colleague restrains him, saying, "That can't be a $100 dollar bill."

"Why not?" asks the younger colleague.

"If it were," comes the reply, "someone would have picked it up by now."

The older economist may have been wrong, of course. Yet his admonition embodies an important truth that people often ignore. The "no cash on the table" principle holds that freely available money seldom sits unclaimed for long. In the future, as in the past, the only way to make real money will be through some combination of talent, thrift, hard work, and luck.

Tens of millions of Americans, however, seem to believe they can get rich in a hurry. They saw others do it in the 1990s simply by transferring their money from old-economy stocks, like General Electric or Procter & Gamble, into Oracle, Cisco Systems, and other high-tech stocks that led the explosive rise of the NASDAQ Index. More recently they saw others get rich overnight by borrowing as much as they could and buying real estate that, by traditional standards, was well beyond their reach.

People who think they can spot cash on the table offer confident explanations for why the usual constraints do not apply. Many bullish stock analysts in the 1990s, for example, insisted that traditional valuation formulas were no longer valid because the Internet was changing the rules of the game. And with business-to-business e-commerce reducing some companies' operating costs by more than 30 percent, there was little doubt that new technologies were creating spectacular productivity gains.

But as everyone now realizes, and should have realized even then, the ultimate value of an e-commerce company depends not on the productivity gains it makes possible but on how much profit it generates. New technologies will continue to generate a burst of profits for companies that are relatively quick to adopt them. But, as in the past, when competitors adopt the same technologies, the long-run savings will be captured not by producers in the form of higher profits but by consumers in the form of lower prices. Thus dairy farmers who were quick to adopt bovine somatotropin, the hormone that increases milk yields by as much as 20 percent, reaped a short-term windfall. But as use of the hormone spread, increased production pushed milk prices steadily downward, eroding profit margins.

A similar profit trajectory ultimately characterized most NASDAQ purveyors of new technologies. Organizers of business-to-business e-commerce may indeed have saved manufacturers hundreds of billions of dollars. But because the new technology companies are no more insulated from competition than dairy farmers, most of those savings took the form of lower product prices, not higher profits.

The no cash on the table principle reminds us to be wary of opportunities that seem too good to be true. It predicted the spectacular NASDAQ crash that occurred in March 2000. But together with the cost-benefit principle, it also helps us understand less spectacular patterns in ordinary markets. Consider, for example, the prices at which products are sold.

Because people's tastes and incomes differ, the amount they are willing to pay for any good typically varies across a broad range. But as Adam Smith argued in *The Wealth of Nations*, the price of a product should not exceed the cost of producing it in the long run. Otherwise, profit opportunities would induce rival sellers to enter the market. And entry would continue until added supply drove price down to cost.

Yet examples abound in which different buyers appear to pay substantially different prices for essentially identical goods and services. These examples seem to contradict the no cash on the table principle. Why doesn't competition from rival sellers force all prices to the same level? Many of the examples we'll take up in Chapter 4 bear directly on this question. For now, suffice to say that in many markets, competition does drive price to a common level.

Within very narrow limits, for example, gold sells for the same price in New York as in London, and for the same price to corporate executives and elementary school teachers. If that were not the case, there would be cash on the table. Suppose, for example, that an ounce of gold sold for $800 in New York and $900 in London. Someone could then buy an ounce of gold in New York and immediately turn a profit of $100 by reselling it in London. The law of one price—which is really just a restatement of the no cash on the table principle—says that the price of gold in the two cities generally will not differ by more than the cost of shipping the stuff from one to the other.

The law of one price applies most forcefully to commodities and services that are sold in perfectly competitive markets. Roughly speaking, these are markets in which numerous suppliers sell highly standardized products. The gold market is a classic example. Gold is a highly standardized commodity, and it is relatively easy for new firms to enter the market whenever and wherever profit opportunities arise.

It is the possibility of arbitrage—purchase at one price with a riskless opportunity to resell at a higher price—that enforces the law of one price. A rich man might be willing to pay more than a poor man for a pound of standard table salt, if only because he has greater ability to pay. Yet the price of salt is the same for all. The law of one price says that any supplier who tried to exploit the rich man's willingness to pay more would create immediate profit opportunities for rival sellers. And even if sellers conspired to maintain higher prices for rich buyers, poor arbitrageurs could stymie their efforts. They could buy salt at the poor man's price and resell it to the rich at a profit by charging just a little less than the rich man's price. As more and more poor men tried to get a piece of this action, the price difference would be driven closer and closer to zero.

The economist's model of supply and demand is essentially a story about the forces that determine which products get produced in which quantities and at what prices. The demand for a given product is a measure of how much people are willing to pay for it. It is a summary, in other words, of the benefits they feel they receive from consuming it. People will keep buying more of a product as long as the value they assign to the last unit consumed is at least as great as its price. The general pattern is that as the price of a good keeps rising, the quantity demanded keeps falling.

The supply of given product is a summary measure of the terms on which producers are willing to offer it for sale. The basic supply rule is that producers will keep offering products for sale as long as the price for which they can sell it is at least as great as their marginal cost—the cost of producing the last unit supplied. In the short run, marginal cost tends to rise with the number of units produced. (This is in part a consequence of the "low-hanging fruit" principle, which says that it is always best to exploit one's best opportunities first.) So on the supply side, the general pattern is that as the price of a good keeps rising, sellers are willing to sell more units.

The market for any given product is said to be in equilibrium when the amount consumers wish to buy at the prevailing price is the same as the amount producers wish to sell. The equilibrium price is also called the *market-clearing price.*

The supply and demand model has enormous power to extract orderly patterns from the cacophony of information that bombards us each day in the marketplace.

Because the market price results when the supply side and the demand side of the market are in balance, it is never correct, strictly speaking, to explain price or quantity movements by referring only to supply or only to demand. Nevertheless, many important patterns in the marketplace can be understood by focusing on sellers in some cases and on buyers in others. The phenomena described in the first sequence of examples are largely driven by the demand (or buyer's) side of the transaction.

Why do many bars charge patrons for water but give them peanuts for free?

Some bars charge their patrons as much as $4 for a half-liter bottle of water, while making sure that full bowls of free salted nuts are always within easy reach. Since nuts are more costly to produce than water, shouldn't it be the other way around?

The key to understanding this practice is to recognize that the terms on which bars offer both water and nuts are dictated by the effect of these commodities on demand for bars' core product, alcoholic beverages. Nuts and alcoholic beverages are complements. Someone who eats more nuts will demand more beer or mixed drinks. Since nuts are relatively cheap and each alcoholic drink generates a relatively high profit margin, making nuts freely available tends to increase bars' profits.

In contrast, water and alcoholic beverages are substitutes. The more water bar patrons drink, the fewer alcoholic beverages they will order. So even though water is relatively inexpensive, bars have an incentive to set a high price for it, thereby discouraging its consumption.

Why do many computer manufacturers offer free software whose market value exceeds the price of the computer itself?

Someone who purchases a new computer today will find that its hard drive already contains not only the latest operating system but also the latest word processing, spreadsheet, presentation, e-mail, music, and photo software, not to mention the latest in virus protection. Why give away all this valuable software?

Software users care a great deal about product compatibility. When scientists or historians are working on a project together, for example, their task will be much simpler if they all use the same word processing program. Likewise, an executive's life will be easier at tax time if her financial software is the same as her accountant's.

A related consideration is that many programs, such as Microsoft Word, are challenging to master. People who become proficient in a program often resist learning another, even if it is objectively better.

The implication is that the benefit of owning and using any given software program increases with the number of other people who use it. This unusual relationship gives the producers of the most popular programs an enormous advantage and makes it hard for new programs to break into the market.

Recognizing this pattern, the Intuit Corporation offered computer makers free copies of Quicken, its personal financial management software. Computer makers were only too happy to include the program, since it made their new computers more attractive to buyers. Quicken soon became the standard for personal financial management programs. By giving away free copies of the program, Intuit "primed the pump," creating an enormous demand for complementary products, such as upgrades of Quicken and more advanced versions of related software. Thus TurboTax and Macintax, Intuit's personal income tax software, have become the standards for tax preparation programs.

Inspired by this success story, other software developers have jumped onto the bandwagon. Some software developers are even rumored to *pay* computer makers to include their programs.

Why does a mobile phone sell for only $39.99, while a spare battery for that same phone sells for $59.99? *(Tianxin Gu)*

If you sign a two-year contract with Verizon in some markets, the company will charge you only $39.99 for a Motorola V120e cell phone. But if you buy an additional battery for your cell phone (perhaps because you expect to be away from your charger for extended periods), you'll pay $59.99. Why must you pay so much more for a replacement battery that is exactly the same as the one in your cheaper cell phone?

Rechargeable lithium ion batteries of the sort used in cell phones are costly to produce. So perhaps the more interesting question is why the original cell phone/battery combination was so cheap. The answer seems to lie in the distinctive cost structure of wireless communication providers. Most of the costs incurred by these companies are fixed costs associated with setting up their networks—constructing cell phone towers, acquiring relevant licenses, and so on. These costs, as well as advertising expenditures, do not vary with the amount of service they provide. The more customers a wireless service provider can attract to help defray these costs, the more likely it is to remain in business.

Suppose the monthly fee for a representative service contract is $50. Any company that manages to sign up one additional customer will then enjoy $600 a year in additional revenue, yet will incur no significant additional costs. Wireless service providers thus face powerful incentives to attract additional customers.

Cell phones and wireless services are strong complements. Experience has demonstrated that offering deeply discounted cell phones is an effective tactic for attracting new customers. Because they buy in bulk, wireless service providers can negotiate deep discounts with Nokia, Motorola, and other cell phone manufacturers. Many companies offer new customers phones for less than they themselves paid for them, and some even provide "free" phones to new customers. But if giving away a phone attracts an additional customer who pays $600 a year in subscription fees, that is a good deal for the wireless company even if it pays Motorola $100 for the phone.

In contrast, offering a discount on spare batteries has not emerged as a successful tactic for attracting new customers. (That is hardly surprising, since most people are not in the market for a spare battery most of the time.) Wireless companies thus find it advantageous to offer cell phones for less than the price of the batteries that power them.

Why are the most expensive apartments in a high-rise building in India those on the upper floors, while the most expensive ones in a low-rise building are those on the lower floors? *(Pankaj Badlani)*

In high-rise apartment buildings in Bombay, the monthly rent for an apartment on a given floor is 1 to 3 percent greater than for a similar apartment one floor down. An apartment on the twentieth floor of a high-rise building might thus rent for 15 to 45 percent more than it would if it were on the fifth floor. In apartment buildings with four stories or fewer, however, the pattern is the reverse. Units on the first and second floors of such buildings rent for significantly more than comparable ones on the third and fourth floors. Why this reversal?

In all cases, a higher apartment offers a better view and reduced street noise. These advantages are clearly greater for apartments atop a high-rise building than for their low-rise counterparts. But even so, it would seem that the advantage of being higher up should command at least some rent premium, irrespective of total building height.

But there is a special twist in India—apartment buildings with four or fewer stories are exempt from the law requiring apartment buildings to have elevators. In low-rise buildings, occupants of apartments on higher floors must thus haul their groceries up several flights of steps. And since the upper-story apartments don't offer dramatic views or even much insulation from street noise, most occupants would choose apartments on the lower floors of low-rise buildings if all rents were the same. The higher demand for such apartments explains why they command higher rents.

Why do many people buy larger houses when they retire and their children leave home? *(Tobin Schilke)*

Many retired people continue living in the house where they raised their family and then move to an assisted-living facility when they can no longer manage on their own. In decades past, when people did relocate after retirement, they typically bought smaller dwellings in Florida, Arizona, or some other location with a mild climate. Many still do, of course. But a recent trend is for retirees to abandon their existing homes in favor of much larger houses close by. Why are they doing this?

One possibility is that current retirees are wealthier and can afford to move into larger houses. But why do they want larger houses after their children leave, and why do they build them close by? After all, they could afford to build or buy a larger dwelling somewhere with a mild climate. Why build a 6,000-square-foot house in Pennsylvania?

A plausible conjecture is that a large house close to grown children's homes may lure the grandchildren to visit more often. With divorce and remarriage more common than in decades past, many children today have six or more grandparents, if the parents of stepparents are in-

Drawing by Mick Stevens.

Large houses for retirees: Grandchildren magnets?

cluded. The demand for visits with grandchildren has thus increased, but the supply of visits has not. So grandparents may hope to increase their share of available visits by building a spacious house that is conveniently located.

Why are hotel prices in Sharm El Sheikh lowest during periods of highest occupancy? *(Rhonda Hadi)*

The normal pattern is for hotel rates to vary directly with occupancy, which in turn varies directly with demand. Occupancy rates for hotels in Sharm El Sheikh, a resort town in Egypt, are substantially higher during the summer months than during the winter months. Why, then, are room prices in Sharm El Sheik significantly lower in the summer months?

Hotel room prices depend on not only occupancy rates but also the willingness and ability of potential occupants to pay for them. Although fewer people visit Sharm El Sheikh during the winter months, they tend to be Europeans and other high-income Westerners. They choose Sharm El Sheikh because its weather promises a respite from chilly northern climates.

In contrast, tourists from Egypt and elsewhere in the Middle East do not face harsh winters and thus prefer to visit in the summer months, when school and work vacations are concentrated. Because these visitors generally have lower incomes than those who visit during winter, hotels are unable to charge the high rates they command in winter.

THE PRECEDING EXAMPLES were explained primarily by differences on the demand side of the market. In each case, the focus was on why buyers might be willing to pay more for one product than another. The examples that follow describe phenomena whose explanation lies primarily on the supply side. In each case, the unexpected price or product offering is linked in some way to differences in cost.

Why do color photographs sell for less than black-and-white ones?
(Othon Roitman)

When baby boomers were growing up, color photographs often cost two or more times as much as standard black-and-white. Today, however, it is black-and-white photos that are more expensive. A photo shop in Ithaca, New York, for example, charges $14.99 to develop and print a thirty-six-exposure roll of black-and-white film but only $6.99 for the same size roll of color film. Why this reversal?

In the 1950s, the consumer market for color photography was in its infancy. Available processes for producing prints from color film were much more complex and costly than the corresponding processes for black-and-white film. Because of this initial cost difference, most people shot photos in black and white, which gave shops an incentive to specialize in that medium. As volume grew, the resulting efficiency gains from specialization further reduced the cost of processing black-and-white photos.

As long as black-and-white continued to be the dominant medium, color processing remained an intrinsically more complex task. But as rising income led more consumers to opt for color, manufacturers developed new optical machines that developed color film and made prints automatically. These machines, which can cost as much as $150,000 apiece, were economical only if a store developed and printed a large volume of photos each day. Their compelling advantage was that they produced a large number of photos with little labor expense. And since labor costs had been the most important component of photo processing costs, stores with the new machines could produce and sell color prints far more cheaply than black-and-white ones.

Why couldn't the same automated machines produce black-and-white photos? Actually they could, but doing so required expensive paper, and the quality of the resulting photos was lower than those processed manually. So over the years, black-and-white photography increasingly became a niche market for professionals and serious amateurs.

Increasingly the norm is to use digital, as opposed to optical, processing machines. Because these machines can print black-and-white photos on the same paper used for color photos, the costs of producing the two types will soon be essentially the same. Once this happens, the premium price for black-and-white photos should disappear.

Why do new cars costing $20,000 rent for $40 a day, while tuxedos costing only $500 rent for around $90? *(John Gotte)*

National rental car chains buy new cars in high volumes and thus are able to negotiate deep discounts from manufacturers. They typically own a car for two years and then sell it for about 75 percent of what they paid for it. So their opportunity cost of owning each car is much lower than a private consumer's would be.

In contrast, most tuxedo rental shops are locally owned and operated. A medium-size location will typically have a rental inventory of a thousand suits, and its annual replacement purchases are not large enough to command deep discounts in purchase prices. Because there is little resale market for used suits, they are often donated or sold for pennies on the dollar to school drama departments and orchestras. So whereas the fees charged by car rental companies must cover about a quarter of the purchase price of each car over a two-year period, tuxedo shops must charge fees that are sufficient to cover the full purchase price of each suit.

More important, the inventory held by rental car companies tends to be more fully utilized than the inventory held by tuxedo shops. Most tuxedo rentals are for events that fall on Saturdays. A shop with a thousand-suit inventory might rent one hundred of its suits on any given Saturday, but on other days of the week consider itself fortunate to rent even five suits. In contrast, a substantial proportion of a rental car company's fleet goes out every day.

Another factor is that rental car companies often collect significantly more than their advertised rates by charging premium prices for add-ons. Insurance surcharges, for example, far exceed the cost of providing insurance, and customers who neglect to fill their gas tanks are charged much more per gallon than normal street prices.

Finally, a tuxedo shop often has to alter a suit to fit the customer and may incur tailoring costs that are almost as high as the rental fee itself. Each suit must be dry-cleaned before it can be rented again, which can add as much as $10 of additional expense for each rental. In contrast, a car rental company need only hose down a returned car before it is ready to go out again.

So even though the retail purchase price of a car is as much as forty times as high as the retail purchase price of a tuxedo, it is not so surprising that the daily rental charge for a car is less than half the fee for a suit.

Why do many cleaners charge more for women's shirts than for men's?
(Don Aday)

Judd Falls Laundromat in Ithaca, New York, charges $5 for washing and pressing a woman's cotton shirt, but only $2 for a man's. Is it discriminating against women?

There is some evidence that women tend to pay more than men for expensive products like cars, whose selling price is usually negotiable. But laundry services do not fall in this category. Laundries typically post different prices for men's and women's garments, and customers almost never attempt to negotiate discounts from these prices.

In general, the more competitive an industry is, the less likely it is to subject customers to discrimination. Even a small town like Ithaca has more than a dozen laundry services listed in the Yellow Pages, which should be more than enough to ensure stiff competition. If existing laundries were charging prices significantly above their cost of processing women's shirts, there would be cash on the table. A rival firm could simply post a sign saying, "No additional charge for women's shirts" and quickly capture most of the women's market.

The persistence of price differentials suggests that they are rooted in differing costs of processing the two types of shirts. As in most service industries, the lion's share of costs incurred by laundries are labor costs. It is hard to imagine how it could be more costly to wash a woman's shirt than a man's. After all, shirts of both types go into the machine and are washed without further handling. So if there is a difference in cost, it must be in pressing the garments. Whenever possible, laundry workers iron shirts on a standard press, which greatly speeds the process. Shirts cannot be pressed on the ironing machine if they are too small or have delicate buttons or detailing. The standard press also clamps the shirt at the bottom, which leaves a conspicuous indentation on the garment. Shirts that cannot be done on a standard press must be done by hand, which takes much longer.

In general the pressing machine accommodates men's shirts better than women's, which are often more delicate and thus more likely to be damaged by the machines. And because women commonly do not tuck their shirts into their pants or skirts, the large indentation left by the pressing machine on the bottom front of the garment is generally considered unacceptable. Men (at least until recently) tend to tuck their shirts in, so the indentation is not problematic for them.

In short, the most plausible explanation for why laundries charge more for women's shirts is that they are more costly, on average, to iron.

Why have Hindi-language movies been attracting much larger audiences in recent years? *(Chris Anderson)*

Until recently, someone from New Delhi living in the United States had to return to India to see movies in his native tongue. But it is now possible even for someone living in Podunk, New York, to choose from hundreds of Hindi-language movie titles. What led to this change?

As Chris Anderson describes in his book *The Long Tail*, traditionally only residents of large cities have had access to foreign-language movie screenings. Theater owners cannot profitably book a film unless scores of paying customers attend each showing. That is a tall order for a Hindi film, even in cities with large populations of Indian immigrants.

With the advent of online DVD distribution services like Netflix, however, the market for relatively obscure movies has been radically transformed. To make money from such movies, it is no longer necessary to attract a significant number of viewers to the same location at the same time. If you want to see *Gol Mol*, a 1979 Hindi comedy featuring Palekar, "a sports-obsessed job seeker whose new boss (Dutt) is a strict disciplinarian who forbids bringing up non-work related topics in the office," you need only add it to your Netflix queue. There is no city in the United States with an Indian population large enough to support theater screenings of *Gol Mol*. But there is a large enough audience for such films to compensate Netflix for the small cost of adding them to its inventory.

Hundreds of thousands of movies and books are insufficiently popular to justify theater screenings or space in a commercial bookstore. The advent of online distribution has rescued these works from extinction.

Why did golf driving ranges spring up all over the suburbs of Washington, D.C., in the early 1990s? *(Charles Kehler)*

With trade associations and lobbyists bidding for real estate in close proximity to the nation's capital, land prices in Washington, D.C., are high. To cover the cost of acquiring a building lot in that market, real estate developers had to charge steep rents. And that generally meant constructing multistory office buildings or apartment houses. Yet dur-

Drawing by Mick Stevens.

The best use of a resource is not always a profitable one.

ing the early 1990s, developers began constructing scores of golf driving ranges. A typical driving range might attract a few dozen customers each evening. Each would pay a few dollars for the privilege of driving golf balls into the night sky, but the total take in any given month would be too small to cover even the interest on the loan required to buy the land. Why did developers use their land in this way?

Washington area developers constructed new office buildings and apartments at a rapid clip throughout the late 1980s. Home prices and office rents had been rising rapidly, and developers had been busily acquiring undeveloped building lots in the expectation of further increases. The upshot is that when the national economic recession began in 1991, the Washington real estate market was substantially overbuilt. Vacancy rates soared and rents plummeted. Any developer who constructed a new office building or housing subdivision during that period could expect it to sit empty for a while.

Instead of building on their undeveloped land, developers could sell it at a depressed price or hold on to it until the market recovered. Those who followed the latter strategy had an obvious incentive to put their land to economic use during the interim. And for that purpose, a golf driving range is almost ideal. All it requires is a stock of used golf balls, a trailer from which to dispense them, and a cart to gather them up. These investments were minimal and would be easy to liquidate when the real estate market recovered.

How could the meager income from a driving range justify the opportunity cost of holding on to land purchased at such great expense? Clearly the developers never would have purchased the land when they did had they anticipated the imminent downturn. But given that they already owned the land and planned to wait out the downturn, their challenge was to make the best possible use of it in the interim. To make economic sense under these circumstances, a driving range need not generate enough revenue to cover the opportunity cost of the land on which it is built. Merely by generating more revenue than the marginal cost of operating them, the driving ranges made developers better off than if they had let their land sit idle.

THE FINAL EXAMPLES in this chapter discuss phenomena whose explanations require attention to both sides of the market, supply and demand.

Why are brown eggs more expensive than white ones? *(Jonathan Chang)*

At Ithaca's largest supermarket, jumbo grade AA eggs sell for $3.09 a dozen if their shells are white but for $3.79 a dozen if their shells are brown. According to the Egg Nutrition Center in Washington, D.C., neither the taste of an egg nor its nutritional quality depends on the color of its shell. What explains this price difference?

It is tempting to say that brown eggs are more expensive because consumers prefer their looks and are willing to pay extra for them. But that observation does not constitute a satisfactory explanation because it seems to imply that sellers of white eggs are leaving cash on the table. If they could earn higher profits by selling brown eggs, why do they continue selling white ones?

A plausible answer is that that brown eggs are more costly to produce than white ones. The color of an egg depends on the breed of hen that lays it. White Leghorn hens, for example, lay white eggs, and Rhode Island Red hens lay brown ones. Brown hens tend to be larger than white ones, and since a hen's daily calorie requirement depends on its size, producing brown eggs costs more. But to explain why they sell for more, an important condition must also be present on the demand side. Unless some consumers prefer the looks of brown eggs and are willing to pay more for them, they will not be offered for sale.

Why would Hallmark give away free "nonoccasion" greeting cards?
(Erik Jepson)

The Hallmark greeting card company recently ran a promotion that offered "nonoccasion" greeting cards for free. The cards, which contained only simple messages like "I'm sorry," "Miss you," and "Good luck," were displayed in a conspicuous, purpose-built, freestanding rack marked with a large sign saying, "Free Cards! Limit Two Per Customer." The cards bore quality artwork and were printed on high-quality stock. They were not overstocks. Nor were they soiled, bent, or damaged in any visible way. And the consumer was not required to purchase other Hallmark merchandise to obtain them. Why was Hallmark giving these cards away?

Greeting cards are extremely high-margin items. Although the marginal production cost is only pennies per card, they often sell for several dollars apiece. The high margins are necessary to help cover the overhead costs of maintaining the retail shops in which they are sold. Apart from birthday cards, whose sales are distributed evenly throughout the year, many of the best-selling types of cards are highly seasonal, such as Christmas and graduation cards. So Hallmark stores are sometimes crowded but most of the time nearly empty. The company could thus increase its profits substantially by finding additional ways to sell cards during off-peak periods.

When the free-card displays appeared, there was no well-established market for nonoccasion greeting cards. Most Hallmark customers were looking to buy cards for birthdays or other specific occasions. Had the company merely offered nonoccasion cards for sale, hardly anyone would have noticed them. But by putting free cards on conspicuous display, the company induced many shoppers to take them home. Hallmark knew that if even a small fraction of these shoppers found satisfying uses for them, it would come out way ahead in the long run. And sure enough, Hallmark now sells nonoccasion cards on essentially the same terms as its seasonal cards. For a seasonal business selling high-margin items, this particular promotion was a big winner.

Why do film processing stores give you a second set of prints for free?
(Laura Sandoval)

When you have a roll of film developed, many stores offer a second set of prints at no additional charge. Yet on any given roll of film, most pictures are not worth duplicating. So why do stores offer free duplicates of the duds, rather than offer the first set of prints at half price?

As noted earlier, most film is now processed automatically. The employee merely loads the roll of negatives and the machine does the rest. To generate a second set of prints, the employee presses a button. No additional labor time is required. The paper and chemicals needed for duplicate prints add to costs, but only slightly. So making two sets of prints costs only a little more.

On the buyer's side, even though most pictures on any given roll are duds, there are inevitably a few that are good enough to send to family or friends. Customers who get a single set of prints must identify the negatives of the pictures they want duplicated and then make an extra trip to the photo store. Duplicates made in this fashion require more care and attention from the equipment operator, so stores must charge high prices to cover their costs.

Stores that offer a second set of prints for free are thus offering a valuable service to their customers at only a minuscule increase in costs. Any store that failed to extend this offer would surely lose many of its customers to competitors.

Why do the most popular books and CDs sell for less than the least popular entries, whereas we observe the opposite pattern for movie ticket prices? *(Ed Varga)*

The list price of Bob Dylan's CD *Modern Times* is $18.99, but when it was released in August 2006 amazon.com sold it for only $8.72, a discount of almost 55 percent. In contrast, recordings by less popular artists are sold at much smaller discounts. For example, Paris Combo's *Motifs* has a list price of $17.98 but is sold on amazon.com for $14.99, a discount of less than 17 percent. The pattern is similar for books. Borders bookstore, for example, offers a 25 percent discount on best-selling books but charges the publisher's suggested retail price for most other titles.

The pattern is the reverse for movie tickets. Although the stated admission price is typically the same for all movies shown at a given time at a given theater, theater owners are much less likely to offer discount coupons for hit movies than for other films. Why are theater operators, but not book and CD sellers, exploiting the fact that buyers are willing to pay more for more popular products?

Each book, movie, and CD is unique. Because rival sellers cannot offer perfect substitutes for these products, the markets for them are not perfectly competitive. Even so, the general pattern in less than perfectly competitive markets is for prices to be higher for products and services that buyers value most highly. This, as noted, is the pattern we observe with movies.

$8.72 $14.99

Are recording artists exempt from the laws of supply and demand?

A plausible explanation for why books and CDs depart from this pattern begins with the observation that the cost conditions for sellers of these products differ sharply from those of theater owners. For theaters, the scarce resource that determines how prices are set is not movies but seats. Once a theater's seats are filled, it is impossible to serve an additional customer at any price. So theater owners have a strong incentive not to offer discounts on films that can fill the seats at the regular admission price. Book and music sellers, in contrast, are unlikely to have to turn away customers if they offer discounts on popular items. Most of the time, they can anticipate which items will be most popular and can accommodate demands by keeping more copies in stock. And since these items turn over rapidly, the per-copy cost of the shelf space required to keep them in stock is very low. Less popular books and CDs, which might sell only a copy or two every few months, generate less revenue for the same shelf space and thus are more costly to keep in stock.

Virtually all retailers stock the most popular books and CDs (since they know there will be a brisk market for them), but there is less overlap in the lists of more obscure entries kept in stock at different stores. And this means retail outlets will face more competitive pressure from one another on the most popular entries. Someone who doesn't like one store's price for a new Dylan CD can buy it at any number of other stores. But few other stores are likely to have the latest Paris Combo CD in stock. Someone who wants that disc right away has little alternative but to pay the supplier's price.

The most successful book and music stores steer their customers to promising but obscure new entries that might otherwise escape their attention. It is thus the least popular titles that are most responsible for the cost of hiring the knowledgeable sales staff required to make these connections. Popular items sell for deeper discounts in part because they are so much cheaper to sell. So the next time you sit down to listen to that great new Paris Combo CD, just remember that you paid more for it than for the popular CDs you can buy at Wal-Mart because your music store bore the additional expense of hiring a salesperson knowledgeable enough to know you'd probably like it.

Yet another impetus for stores to discount best-selling books and CDs is that the practice attracts additional customers to stores, who are likely to buy other items.

Why don't top-ranked private universities charge higher tuition than many of their lower-ranked counterparts? *(Lonnie Fox)*

Annual tuition payments vary within a remarkably narrow band across universities ranked among the top 100 private institutions by the *U.S. News and World Report*. Yet the demand for positions in the entering freshman class is far more intense at the top-ranked schools in this group than at their lesser-ranked counterparts. In one recent year, for example, a top-ranked school admitted less than 10 percent of the students who applied, whereas many lower-ranked schools admit 50 percent or more of their applicants. The expenditures per pupil are also higher at the top-ranked universities. If both costs and demand are higher at top-ranked universities, why don't they charge more?

Although there can be only ten universities ranked in the top 10 at any given moment, there are usually fifty more whose administrators firmly believe they would have made the top 10 if not for some shortcoming in the rankings formulas. And with the full blessing of faculty, students, and alumni, administrators spare little effort to improve their institution's standing in the eyes of external evaluators. Considerable rewards accrue to all these groups when a university achieves elite status.

To be a realistic candidate for such status, a university must attract a world-class student body. Many of the rankings formulas give explicit weight to the average SAT scores of a school's entering freshman class. The upshot is that top universities are forced to compete bitterly for their most talented students. The select few to whom they grant admission are also much in demand by other top-ranked schools.

Harvard would have no trouble filling its freshman class with reasonably qualified students even if its tuition were $100,000 a year. But if it charged that much, it would attract only a fraction of the top students it attracts today. Many parents would ask, "Why pay $100,000 to send my children to Harvard when I can send them to Princeton for only $40,000?"

Tuition payments cover only a fraction—in many cases, less than one-third—of the total cost of educating a student. Most of the rest comes from endowments and annual gifts from alumni and others. Top-ranked institutions are able to cover the higher costs they incur because their income from gifts and endowments tends to be much larger than at lesser-ranked institutions.

The result is an equilibrium in which students pay no more to attend the highest-ranked school than to attend the number 100 school. The top-ranked school cannot charge more because it needs its most accomplished students every bit as much as they need it.

3

Why Equally Talented Workers Often Earn Different Salaries and Other Mysteries of the World of Work

The labor market is the most important one most of us will ever participate in. Although people themselves cannot be sold in markets, selling human services is perfectly legal. The market for these services is subject to the same laws of supply and demand that apply in product markets. When the supply of carpenters increases, carpenters' wage rates tend to fall. If the demand for computer programmers rises, we expect their wage rates to rise.

The first example we'll consider in this chapter illustrates the fundamental principle of competitive labor markets—workers tend to be paid in rough proportion to the value they add to their employer's bottom line.

Why do female models earn so much more than male models? *(Fran Adams)*

Fashion model Heidi Klum earned $7.5 million in 2005, and several other top female models earned even more, topped by Gisele Bündchen at more than $15 million. Five female supermodels made *Forbes Magazine*'s list of

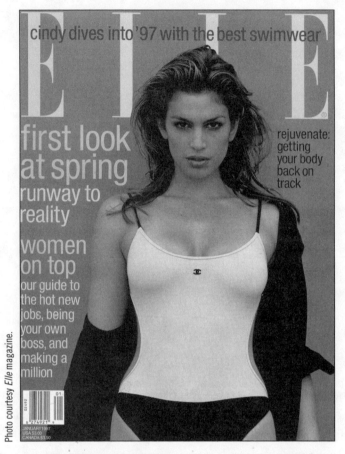

Photo courtesy *Elle* magazine.

Cindy Crawford, the highest-paid supermodel of the 1990s. Even today, no male model earns nearly as much.

the one hundred highest-paid celebrities that year. No male models made the list. Why are the top female models paid so much more?

To answer this question, we must first ask what fashion models accomplish for the clothing producers who hire them. Simply put, their job is to make the manufacturer's apparel look as good as possible to prospective buyers. Since most clothing looks better on attractive people, manufacturers seek out the best-looking male and female models for their photo shoots. So among both male and female models, the better-looking models are generally paid more. And since society has its own standard of beauty for each sex, it makes little sense to say that female models are paid more because they are better-looking than their male counterparts.

Female models receive premium pay because women's fashion is a vastly bigger business than men's fashion. Women in the United States, for example, spend more than twice as much on clothing each year as men do, and the difference is even more pronounced in other countries. With such large sums at stake, bidding aggressively for the model who best conveys the look of the moment makes economic sense for manufacturers of women's clothing. Widely read fashion magazines such as *Vogue* and *Elle* have enormous influence on women's clothing and cosmetics purchases. Each issue contains photographs of hundreds or even thousands of female models. Those who can capture the reader's attention against that crowded backdrop are worth their weight in gold. So it is easy to see why manufacturers might be willing to bid a lot more for a model who stands out even slightly from the field.

The value added by hiring a better-looking male model pales by comparison. Few men could even name a men's fashion magazine, and fewer still read one. The clothing manufacturer that hires a slightly better-looking male model will sell additional garments, but not nearly as many more as the one that hires a slightly better-looking female model.

Women are also hired to model cosmetics, and here too the payoff from hiring a more striking model can be enormous. Because most men don't wear cosmetics, few male models participate in that segment of the labor market.

Why have top earners' salaries been growing so much faster than everyone else's?

During the three decades following World War II, incomes grew at almost the same rate—just under 3 percent annually—for people up and down the income ladder. Since then, however, most income gains have gone to those at the top. Thus, although the median wage is about the same now, in purchasing power terms, as in 1975, the top 1 percent of earners now make roughly three times as much as they did then. Higher up, the gains have been even larger. CEOs of the largest American corporations, for example, now earn more than five hundred times as much as the average worker, up from forty-two times as much in 1980. Why this shift?

Although many factors are involved, one in particular stands out—the rapid acceleration of technological changes that increase the leverage of the most able individuals. Conditions are different in every industry, but the tax advice industry provides an illustrative case in point.

In the 1970s, that industry was dominated almost entirely by local accountants. The most talented accountants earned more than their colleagues, but income differences were generally modest. Then came a wave of national tax advice franchises, such as H&R Block, whose organizers discovered that the lion's share of tax returns could be completed successfully by nonprofessionals guided by a relatively small number of experts. Fueled by effective national advertising, these firms shifted demand away from local accountants, creating enormous income gains for franchise organizers.

More recently, people have begun relying on computer software to guide them through their tax returns. Scores of these programs initially competed for buyers' attention, but once critics identified Intuit's TurboTax and a few others as the most comprehensive and user-friendly entries in this tournament, the market for competing programs quickly evaporated. Once the code has been written for the best tax software program, additional copies of it can be produced at zero marginal cost, which renders lesser programs economically irrelevant. So if we compare the current tax advice industry to its counterpart from the 1970s, the losers have been local accountants, while the big winners have been the organizers of the firms that produce the leading software programs, such as Intuit's TurboTax.

CEO pay has escalated for similar reasons. Modern information technologies, together with lower transportation costs and tariff barriers, have increased the scope of markets. A tire company once could have survived by being the best manufacturer in Ohio but today must be among a handful of the most efficient producers worldwide. With markets so much broader in scope and so much more competitive than in the past, small differences in the quality of executive decisions now translate into much bigger differences in corporate earnings.

Greater leverage and competition, of course, do not explain all increases in executive pay. As the Enron and WorldCom examples made clear, some executives have relied on accounting fraud to increase their wealth. But studies suggest that salary gains at the top have occurred primarily because executive decisions have become much more important to the bottom line.

IN PRODUCT MARKETS, the price of a good depends on its attributes. A high-definition TV, for example, commands a higher price than a conventional one. The same is true in labor markets, where the wage associated with a given job will depend on its characteristics. What economists call the theory of compensating wage differentials was originally advanced by Adam Smith in *The Wealth of Nations:*

> The whole of the advantages and disadvantages of the different employments of labour and stock, must, in the same neighbourhood, be either perfectly equal, or continually tending to equality. If, in the same neighbourhood, there was any employment evidently either more or less advantageous than the rest, so many people would crowd into it in the one case, and so many would desert it in the other, that its advantages would soon return to the level of other employments. . . . Every man's interest would prompt him to seek the advantageous, and to shun the disadvantageous employment.

Smith's theory thus explains why, when all other relevant factors are the same, wages will be higher in jobs that are more risky, require more arduous effort, or are located in ugly or smelly locations. The next examples illustrate other, perhaps less expected, consequences of the theory of compensating wage differentials.

Why are people who repave driveways paid only half as much in the suburbs of Dallas as in the suburbs of Minneapolis? *(Danielle Routt)*

Shortly after moving into a home in suburban Dallas, the owner obtained an estimate for repaving her driveway, a job she had done at the house she had just sold in suburban Minneapolis. Much to her surprise, the estimate she was given in Dallas called for almost exactly the same amount she previously spent for materials but only half as much for labor. Why was labor so much cheaper in Dallas?

According to the law of one price, jobs with identical skill requirements and working conditions should pay the same wage. The skills required to repave a driveway are essentially the same in Minneapolis as in Dallas, and repaving a driveway requires essentially the same effort in both locations. But other working conditions are not equally attractive in both locations. In particular, the relatively mild Dallas climate enables paving contractors to work steadily throughout the year, whereas the harsh winters of Minneapolis prevent them from working for several months. (It is said that there are two seasons in Minneapolis: winter and July.) If winter meant only a few weeks of enforced idleness, that might not be seen as a handicap. But being unable to work for months on end would severely limit the ability of contractors to survive if they earned the same wage as in Dallas.

According to Adam Smith's theory of compensating wage differentials, wages adjust so that the overall conditions of employment tend toward equality across jobs that demand similar skills. If conditions are more attractive in one job than another, wages in the first job will thus tend to adjust in the opposite direction. One of the desirable conditions that Smith specifically mentioned was "constancy of employment." This feature helps explain why contractors' wages in Minneapolis are substantially higher than in Dallas. Higher wages are needed to compensate Minnesota contractors for their inability to ply their trade during the winter months.

Wage differences between the two cities are further accentuated by the fact that the shorter work season in Minneapolis serves to concentrate demand, since people who want their driveways done in a given year must do it in the same five or six months.

Why are servers paid more than assistant chefs at high-end restaurants?
(Lesley Viles)

A server in an expensive restaurant can earn several hundred dollars an evening in tips alone, while an assistant chef in the same restaurant can expect to earn only a small fraction of that. Although both jobs are important for the restaurant's success, most people agree that the experience, talent, and training required to become a good assistant chef are in shorter supply than the qualities required of a good server. So why is the server paid much more?

The pay that any given job commands depends on many factors besides the skills it requires. Many highly skilled jobs pay relatively little because they are seen as stepping-stones to other desirable jobs. The assistant chef's position falls into this category, but the server's does not. Highly skilled people are willing to work as assistant chefs at relatively low pay because the position provides essential training and experience for becoming a head chef, a respected and well-paid post.

A waiter's position, in contrast, is a terminal slot. Many waiters never go on to higher-paying jobs, and those who do typically do not owe their subsequent success to their background as waiters.

Why are CEOs of large tobacco companies willing to testify under oath that nicotine is not addictive?

On April 14, 1994, the CEOs of seven large American tobacco companies were sworn in before a congressional committee hearing on the regulation of tobacco products. One by one, the CEOs proclaimed their belief that nicotine is not addictive. In the light of widely available scientific evidence that nicotine is in fact highly addictive, these CEOs were scorned and ridiculed for their testimony. Why were they willing to endure this humiliation?

Having to endure public humiliation would certainly appear to qualify as an undesirable condition of employment under Adam Smith's theory of compensating wage differentials. And sure enough, tobacco CEOs are among the highest paid executives in the country. For

Photo by Stephen Crowley / New York Times.

Tobacco executives: Higher salaries for an unpalatable task?

example, Altria, the parent company of the Philip Morris cigarette companies, paid its CEO $18.13 million in 2005.

Why are the least productive workers in a work group within a firm typically paid more than the value of what they produce, while the most productive workers are paid less?

The theory of competitive labor markets suggests that workers will be paid in accordance with the value of what they produce for their employers. Yet in most organizations, productivity appears to vary much more across employees doing similar jobs than wages do. The top-ranked workers appear to be paid less in proportion to what they contribute, while the bottom-ranked workers are paid more. This seems like a good deal for the bottom-ranked workers. But if the top-ranked workers are in fact underpaid, why aren't they bid away by some other employer who will pay them their due?

At first glance, this pattern seems to imply cash on the table. If the top-ranked worker in a firm is worth $100,000 and is being paid only $70,000, then a rival firm could pocket a quick $20,000 in extra profits by luring her away at a salary of $80,000. But this would still leave cash on the table for other rival firms. So her salary should be quickly bid up to $100,000, if that's the value of what she contributes.

A possible explanation for why the observed pattern of wages might be stable begins with the assumption that most workers would prefer to occupy high-ranked positions in their work groups than low-ranked ones. But not every worker's preference for a high-ranked position can be satisfied within any given work group. After all, 50 percent of the positions in the group must always be in the bottom half. So the only way some workers are able to enjoy the satisfaction inherent in positions of high rank is if others are willing to endure the dissatisfactions associated with low rank. If workers cannot be forced to remain with an organization against their wishes, the low-ranked workers will find it attractive to remain only if they receive additional compensation.

Where does this extra compensation come from? It appears to be financed by an implicit tax on the earnings of their high-ranked coworkers. If the tax isn't too high, the high-ranked workers are happy to remain with the firm, even though they could earn more elsewhere, and the low-ranked workers find the extra pay sufficient to compensate for the burdens of low rank. The resulting pay pattern in each firm is the functional equivalent of a progressive income tax.

In many occupations, individuals face a menu of job choices in different firms. Those who don't care much about having high local rank do best by accepting low-ranked positions at premium pay in firms with highly productive employees. Others who place high value on high local rank do best by accepting high-ranked positions at lower pay in firms with lower average productivity.

ALTHOUGH THE MARKET for labor shares many features with markets for goods like cash registers and printing presses, there are also important differences. For instance, employers need not worry that a printing press will take too many coffee breaks or steal from the office supply cabinet. As the following examples illustrate, these differences explain many interesting wage patterns and employment practices.

Why do we leave tips for some services but not for others? *(Dolapo Enaharo)*

When people go out for dinner in the United States, it is customary to leave the server who provides good service a tip of 15 to 20 percent of the total bill. But the providers of many other services have no expectation of receiving tips. And it is actually illegal to tip some service providers. Why this distinction?

Tipping in restaurants is thought to have been introduced as a means of encouraging better service. Restaurant owners are willing to pay their servers higher wages if they provide attentive and courteous service because diners who have an enjoyable experience are more likely to come back. Servers, for their part, would be willing to expend the extra effort in return for higher pay. The problem is that it is difficult for owners to monitor the quality of table service directly. Reducing the price of the meal slightly and announcing that diners should leave a little extra for the server if they are pleased with their service helps solve this problem. Diners, after all, are perfectly positioned to monitor service quality. And since most diners patronize the same restaurants repeatedly, a server who receives a generous tip for good service on one occasion will typically provide even better service on the diner's next visit.

Competitive pressures in the restaurant industry make it difficult for servers to exploit customers by withholding good service from those who don't offer extravagant tips. If they tried, people would exercise their option to dine elsewhere.

But in other contexts, customers do not enjoy similar protection. Unhappy motorists, for example, do not have the option of taking their business elsewhere if they receive unsatisfactory service from a clerk at the Department of Motor Vehicles. People typically do not visit the DMV unless they have to. And while it might be nice to enjoy better service at the DMV, we are understandably reluctant to empower DMV clerks to demand tips as a precondition for serving us.

Why do many fast food restaurants promise a free meal if you are not given a receipt at the time of purchase? *(Sam Tingleff)*

Most people who eat at fast food restaurants are not traveling on expense accounts and are thus unlikely to require meal receipts for reimbursement. Why, then, do so many fast food restaurants post signs next to their cash registers advising diners that their meals will be free if they are not offered receipts when they pay for them?

To deter theft, owners of restaurants and other retail establishments require cashiers to reconcile the total amount of cash collected during their shift with the total volume of sales rung up at their register. If the amount of cash falls short, cashiers are typically responsible for making up the difference.

Monitoring employees: The customer often has the clearest view.

One way cashiers can circumvent this control is by neglecting to ring up a proportion of their transactions. This tactic works because it is difficult to match specific changes in a restaurant's food inventory with individual transactions at any given cash register. Thus if a cashier failed to ring up a customer's $20 meal, he or she could pocket the $20 without creating an accounting discrepancy at the end of the day.

Owners could hire supervisors to verify that cashiers ring up every sale. But that would be expensive. By offering a complimentary meal to anyone who fails to receive a receipt, owners provide an economic incentive for customers to monitor cashiers for free.

Why does a worker's wage often rise more quickly over time than his or her productivity? (Edward Lazear)

A common pattern in firms that offer long-term employment is that an employee's wage rises each year by more than his or her increase in productivity. Assuming that average pay cannot exceed average productivity over the course of the worker's career with the firm, it follows that employees in such firms are paid less than they are worth during the early years of their tenure, and more than they are worth during their later years. But why would a firm retain an employee once her wage became greater than she was worth?

One explanation for the observed time profile of wages is that it functions, in effect, as a device for preventing workers from cheating and shirking. In the United States alone, employee malfeasance costs firms billions of dollars each year. If firms could find ways of reducing it, they could pay their employees more and earn higher profits at the same time. The potential attraction of a wage schedule that rises faster than productivity is that a dishonest or lazy worker would be unwilling to accept employment under a contract like this. Even though the lifetime value of wages might be high under the contract, wages in the early years are lower than could be obtained elsewhere, and a dishonest worker would have reason to fear being caught and fired before becoming eligible for premium pay. In contrast, honest workers could accept work under the same contract and feel secure that they would maintain their positions long enough to reap the delayed bonuses. Firms, for their part, know that failure to maintain a reputation for honoring the contract would jeopardize their ability to hire new workers.

Why do employers sometimes offer wages that are higher than necessary to attract the quality and quantity of labor they wish to hire? *(George Akerlof)*

The theory of competitive labor markets says that employers will offer wages only as high as necessary to attract the workforce they desire. Yet it is common at many firms to see scores of highly qualified applicants for every vacant position. Couldn't these firms earn higher profits by paying less?

One possibility is that offering premium wages creates a bond that helps ensure honest behavior on the part of employees. A worker who was paid only the going rate would have little reason to worry about losing his job. In perfectly competitive labor markets, after all, jobs are more or less readily available at the going rate. But jobs at premium wages are not freely available. So a worker fortunate enough to land one will have strong economic incentives to do whatever he can to keep it. In particular, he is less likely to shirk than his counterpart in a job that pays only the going rate. If the disincentive for shirking is strong enough, it enables the firm to remain profitable despite the burden of paying premium wages.

Why do most companies conduct background checks before extending an employment offer, whereas most MBA programs conduct background checks only after applicants are accepted? *(Okwu Njoku)*

It is customary for large corporations to hire private companies to conduct background checks on job applicants before extending job offers. Many universities conduct similar background checks on people admitted to professional degree programs. But unlike the company background checks, the university background checks typically occur after applicants have been admitted. Why don't business schools investigate applicants to their MBA programs before deciding whether to admit them?

One possibility is that the cost of hiring the wrong person in business is much greater than the cost of admitting the wrong applicant to an MBA program. But if so, why would MBA programs conduct costly background checks at all?

The recruitment process for professional degree programs differs from the recruitment process for large corporations. People who are seeking admission to professional degree programs often apply to a dozen different institutions at once—three or four "reach" schools, another half dozen for which their odds of acceptance are reasonably good, plus a couple of safety schools. As a result, most institutions know that a high proportion of their accepted applicants will matriculate someplace else. People seeking employment in large corporations may also apply to several organizations, but as the interview process unfolds over time, they are unlikely to remain serious candidates for more than one or two positions. Background checks are expensive. MBA programs that conduct these checks typically do them only after they have reasonably firm evidence—such as a deposit check in hand—that an accepted applicant intends to matriculate.

MOST JOBS REQUIRE EMPLOYEES to work a specified schedule of hours each week in return for a fixed weekly salary that is agreed on in advance. But in some jobs, workers get paid only when they sell their services directly to the public. The next two examples illustrate the kinds of decisions workers confront in such jobs.

Why do independent musicians, especially the most talented ones, favor free music-sharing programs, while established star performers tend to oppose them? (Kelly Bock, Chris Frank)

When Napster introduced the first Internet music file-sharing program in 1999, established stars like Metallica and Madonna were quick to condemn it. In contrast, many aspiring independent musicians applauded file sharing. Why were independent musicians so eager to see their songs given away?

Because established stars earn a substantial share of their income from the sale of CDs, it seems hardly surprising that many of them opposed giving consumers free access to their music. But the incentives facing independent musicians are markedly different. These musicians can never expect significant sums from CD sales without first creating at least a strong regional fan base. And with tens of thousands of aspiring indie bands competing for access to a limited number of performance venues, the odds of achieving even that level of success are remote. Granted, a good enough band could expect to become popular in its local music market eventually. But the real hurdle has always been the move from local to regional popularity, and file sharing appears to have made that move more meritocratic. Because local fans can now e-mail songs to friends in nearby cities, it is more likely that the best bands will garner bookings in venues outside their home markets.

Even with its music available on the Internet for free, an indie band that achieves a threshold level of regional popularity can expect to earn significant income from the sale of CDs. Diehard music fans who would feel no qualms about downloading free music from artists signed to major commercial labels are often willing to purchase the CDs of their favorite indie bands.

In short, the observed reactions to music file sharing make economic sense. Established stars stand to lose from it on balance, and aspiring indie musicians—especially the best ones—stand to gain.

Why do taxi drivers quit early on rainy days? *(Linda Babcock, Colin Camerer, George Loewenstein, and Richard Thaler)*

In most big cities, it is possible to hail a taxi at a moment's notice when the weather is good. But when it's raining, people have a much harder time finding one. One obvious reason is that many people who walk short distances during good weather prefer to take a cab in the rain. So any given fleet of taxis will tend to be more fully occupied on rainy days. But the supply of available taxis is also smaller because taxi drivers work shorter hours when it rains. Why?

According to a recent survey, the reason is that many taxi drivers work only as long as it takes to reach a targeted income each day. On sunny days, they must spend much of their day cruising for fares, so it

Photo by Chris Frank.

By quitting early when it rains, taxi drivers miss their biggest paydays.

takes longer to reach the target. They can reach the target more quickly when it's raining because cabs tend to be full most of the time.

That taxi drivers knock off earlier on rainy days is precisely the opposite of what their economic incentives might seem to favor. After all, the opportunity cost of quitting an hour sooner is much lower on sunny days than on rainy days. If their goal were to reach a target level of income over a longer period—say, one month—by working the smallest possible number of hours, cab drivers should work as many hours as possible on rainy days and take more time off on sunny days.

UNLESS THE OPPORTUNITY COST of your time is zero, it costs you something to mow your own lawn and iron your own shirts. Both people and firms must decide which services to perform for themselves and which to delegate to outside contractors. The following examples illustrate how these "make/buy" decisions play out in different settings.

Why has it become more common to hire a professional to change a flat tire? (Timothy Alder)

When a student recently polled sixteen members of his extended family about whether they knew how to change a flat tire, nine said they could not, and the remaining seven said they could, although several admitted never having done so. There was also a clear pattern to the responses: the nine who said they could not change a tire were younger than the seven who thought they could. Why does the ability to change a flat tire seem to be disappearing?

As usual, the economic naturalist attempts to answer such questions by examining changes in the relevant costs and benefits. The cost of learning how to change a flat tire does not appear to have changed appreciably during the past generation. If anything, it may have gone down slightly because of design improvements in the jacks used to raise wheels off the pavement.

But significant changes have occurred in the benefit of learning how to change a flat tire. One is that improved tire design has made flat tires much less common than in the past. Many cars now even have run-flat tires, which enable cars to be driven safely even when tire pressure is extremely low. Another significant change is that most people now carry cell phones when they drive, enabling them to summon a repair service even in remote locations.

On both counts, the benefits of knowing how to change a flat tire are smaller than they once were. Better tires have made it less likely that this skill will ever be called on, and if a flat should occur, summoning help is easier. Because of such changes, many younger drivers seem to have decided that the benefit of learning how to change a flat tire no longer exceeds the cost.

Why do companies hire temporary management consultants at premium rates rather than hiring full-time managers at much lower salaries? (James Balet)

When companies engage the services of management consulting firms, they must pay for not only the consultants' time but also the substantial overhead fees levied by consulting companies. Some of these companies collect three dollars in fees for every dollar in salary they pay the consultants. Why don't client companies save money by hiring additional managers directly?

One possible explanation is that management consulting services are analogous to the expensive generators that electric power companies employ to meet peak demand. These utilities serve the bulk of their loads with baseload generators, which are costly to buy but relatively cheap to operate. It does not pay to serve demands of short duration with this expensive equipment, because it would sit idle most of the time. So utilities serve short bursts of demand with peakers, which are more expensive to run, but much cheaper to buy, than baseload equipment.

Similarly, the demand for managerial services within any company is never perfectly level over time. Most companies may thus find it prudent to hire their own full-time managers to provide most of their day-to-day managerial services and hire management consultants to meet peak needs for brief periods. True, each hour of consulting costs much more than each hour of management provided by an in-house employee. But if peak periods of demand for managerial services are sufficiently brief, it may nonetheless be cheaper to provide many of those services with expensive consultants. The alternative, after all, would be to hire additional in-house managers who would sit idle most of the time.

A second possibility is that companies may be willing to pay premium prices to management consultants because they know that controversial business strategies are often easier to implement if initiated by respected external advisers. A company may know, for example, that weak sales forecasts dictate laying off a proportion of its workforce but may fear taking that step because of its effect on the morale of remaining employees. In such cases, it may be easier to tell workers that the layoffs were not management's idea but a recommendation from McKinsey.

Why might an electric utility keep an expensive outside attorney on permanent retainer, when it could hire that same attorney for less than half the price?

An electric utility in upstate New York pays more than $1 million a year in fees to a Chicago law firm in return for the full-time services of the firm's senior attorney. The law firm pays that attorney an annual salary of less than $500,000. Why doesn't the electric utility save itself half a million dollars a year by hiring the lawyer directly?

As regulated companies, electric utilities employ large permanent staffs of attorneys to handle their cases before regulatory agencies. Because most of these cases are routine, the in-house attorneys who manage them can often be hired for less than $100,000 a year. But a small proportion of the utility's legal caseload involves very high stakes. For these cases, even small differences in legal talent can mean a difference of millions of dollars a year in shareholder profits. The utility thus has a clear interest in hiring top legal talent to oversee these cases, even if it means paying extremely high salaries.

But hiring an in-house attorney at a salary of $500,000 a year would inevitably kindle increased salary demands from in-house attorneys who make less. When the cost of dealing with these demands is factored in, it may end up being cheaper to pay the attorney $1 million as an outside consultant.

THE FINAL EXAMPLE in this chapter illustrates that the ways professionals are compensated for their services may affect the kinds of advice they offer.

Why might a patient with a sore knee be more likely to receive an MRI exam if he has conventional health insurance than if he belongs to an HMO?

Under conventional health insurance contracts, doctors are reimbursed according to prearranged fee schedules for each service they deliver for their patients. The more services they perform, the more they are paid.

In contrast, the standard HMO consists of a group of physicians who charge each patient a fixed annual fee. In return the physicians agree to provide whatever services they believe to be in the best interests of their patients. Under HMO contracts, physicians are thus paid the same amount per patient no matter how many services the patient receives.

Most physicians undoubtedly attempt to meet their patients' health needs as best they can, irrespective of which kind of contract they work under. But there are always ambiguous cases. A patient with a sore knee, for example, might see improvement from simply resting the joint for a few weeks. But a costly MRI exam might reveal structural damage best treated by surgery. In such cases, the fact that HMO physicians bear the cost of the test—not to mention the ensuing surgery, if indicated—will inevitably predispose some to favor a wait-and-see strategy. A physician treating the same patient under conventional health insurance would have a much stronger incentive to order the test immediately.

4

Why Some Buyers Pay More Than Others

The Economics of Discount Pricing

T he law of one price applies most forcefully in perfectly competitive markets—roughly speaking, markets like those for salt or gold in which numerous suppliers sell highly standardized products. But many products are not sold in perfectly competitive markets. For example, although films in a given genre may seem interchangeable, local movie screenings are not standardized products. Different theater locations and start times make each showing unique in at least some respects. And few moviegoers would regard *Casablanca* as a perfect substitute for *Scary Movie VIII*.

Because the law of one price does not apply in the market for film screenings, economists are not surprised that movie tickets do not all sell for the same price. Matinees, for example, are generally priced lower than evening showings of the same film because fewer people are free to attend movies in the afternoon than in the evening.

Theater owners also offer discounts to specific groups of people—students and senior citizens, for example—whose demands are believed to be more sensitive to price. Unlike gold or salt, movie tickets cannot be freely resold. A young person cannot buy a student ticket and make a profit by reselling it to an adult because the discount ticket is valid only for patrons with a student ID. When the seller is offering an experience, not a tangible product, opportunities for arbitrage are inherently limited. It wouldn't work, for example, for a student to watch a movie and then try to resell the experience to an adult.

But in markets for tangible products—especially expensive ones—the possibility of arbitrage limits the ability of even monopolists to charge higher prices to some buyers than others. For women who will wear only Manolo Blahnik shoes, for instance, Blahnik is a pure monopolist. Even so, the possibility of resale transactions among buyers limits that firm's ability to tailor its prices to each individual's willingness to pay. Similarly, theater owners would find it difficult to charge adults $5 for popcorn while charging students only $2, since nothing would prevent students from buying popcorn at the discount price and reselling it at a profit to adults.

Although the possibility of arbitrage often limits the ability to charge different prices for the same product, sellers have developed ingenious ways of getting around this constraint. Many of these tricks have a common feature: the seller permits the buyer to purchase at a discount, but only if the buyer is first willing to jump a hurdle of some sort. The most common example is the temporary sale. Those who are willing to spend the effort can obtain a discount by becoming aware of when the sale takes place and taking the trouble to buy during that window. Those who are unwilling to take those steps pay a higher price.

Once you see a few examples of the hurdle method of differential pricing, you will seldom encounter products whose sellers do not employ some version of it. Some years ago, I traveled to Minneapolis to attend a conference. Before departing, I had made a reservation in a hotel whose daily room rate was equivalent to about $200 at today's prices. As I was checking in, I noticed a sign behind the clerk saying, "Ask about our special rates." Curious, I asked and was told that I could have the room for $150.

The hurdle I had to jump to be eligible for that discount was to ask a simple question. Since it was such an easy hurdle to clear, it's natural to wonder if any patrons failed to ask. But when I put that question to the front desk clerk, he told me that most people did not bother.

A discount hurdle is effective from the seller's point of view if potential buyers who are highly price sensitive (and probably would not purchase the product without the discount) find the hurdle easy to jump, while others who are not sensitive to price find it hard or simply not worth their while. In my case, the sign inviting customers to ask about special rates ended up costing the hotel $50. Still, it may have been an effective hurdle for some guests who had not registered in advance. Certain guests would find it unseemly to inquire about a special rate, and such guests are rarely very sensitive to price. Others, such as business travelers on expense accounts, simply might not care.

The first two examples in this chapter illustrate specific methods of hurdle discount pricing.

Why are hotel minibar prices so exorbitant? *(Kem Wilson)*

If you want a liter bottle of Evian mineral water from the minibar at the Parker Meridien Hotel in Manhattan, you'll have to pay four dollars for it. But if you're willing to walk to the Duane Reade drugstore around the corner, you can buy it for ninety-nine cents. Why are markups on hotel minibar items so steep?

A dedicated retail establishment can sell almost any item for less than a nonspecialist would have to charge. After all, the retail establishment sells in high volume and is able to take advantage of efficiencies of specialization. That might account for a hotel having to charge as much as $2 to cover its costs of selling a bottle of water that a drugstore could sell for $1. But the hotel's costs could not conceivably be four times a drugstore's.

More plausibly, minibar prices are so high because the sale of these items provides an indirect means for the hotel to target discounts to price-sensitive buyers. In order to achieve high occupancy rates, hotels are under pressure to offer their rooms at competitive prices. Many hotels, for example, offer lower rates for rooms booked on the Internet, which is consistent with evidence that Internet shoppers are more price sensitive than others.

Because the hotel industry is highly competitive, hotels do not enjoy especially high profit margins. To offer deeper discounts to price-sensitive guests, a hotel must thus find ways of collecting additional revenue from other guests. Hotels know perfectly well that offering minibar items at inflated prices ensures that many guests will buy nothing from the minibar. But they also know that guests who are less price sensitive will not be deterred by high minibar prices. The added profits that hotels reap from these guests permit them to offer deeper discounts on room rates. The discount hurdle in this case is having to forgo the convenience of minibar purchases. Taking that step confers eligibility for the lower hotel bills that premium minibar prices make possible.

Why is it more expensive to transfer funds between banks electronically than send a check through the mail? *(Selin Doganeli)*

If someone owes you $10,000, you have at least two choices for how to transfer the money from her bank to yours. She can send you a check, and your bank will deposit it to your account at no charge. Or she can instruct her bank to wire the money to your account, in which case your bank will charge you a fee, often $15 for domestic transfers. Why does your bank charge for receiving an electronic funds transfer, even though processing a check deposit is actually more expensive?

Processing a check entails the handling, scanning, and often shipment of paper documents. Several days may elapse before the money is actually credited to your account. With an electronic funds transfer, in contrast, everything happens more or less at the speed of light. An employee in one bank enters the relevant information into a computer, and the amounts in both the host and recipient accounts are adjusted instantaneously.

Banks charge more for electronic transfers because customers who choose to transfer money that way reveal by so doing that speedy transfer is of significant value to them. Check transfers tend to be for smaller amounts, so the delays involved in gaining access to the money are typically of little consequence. Electronic transfers, in contrast, tend to involve larger sums. They are often funds needed to complete urgent business transactions. Because consumers value the speed of such transactions, banks have discovered that they can charge significant fees for them.

Waiting for a check to clear before being able to spend your money is thus a hurdle you can jump in order to avoid the fee for transferring money electronically.

Efficiency Gains from Discount Pricing

Imagine every student in a third grade class being sent outside to form a line with the tallest student in front, followed by the second tallest student, and so on. Then imagine students filing back into the classroom from the head of the line, one student every five minutes. As the classroom filled up, what would happen to the average height of students in the room with each new arrival? Because each arriving student would be shorter than the ones already there, the average height of the assembled students would clearly fall with each new arrival.

This pattern is similar to a cost pattern that has important implications for pricing patterns in the marketplace. In many production processes, marginal cost (again, the economist's term for the cost of producing one additional unit) is lower than average cost—the producer's total cost divided by the total number of units produced. This cost structure is characteristic of production processes said to exhibit "economies of scale." For such processes, average cost continues to fall as the number of units produced increases, just as average height falls when each arriving student is shorter than the ones before.

To survive in the long run, producers must sell their output at prices that, on average, are at least as great as their average cost of production. (If the average price per unit sold were less than average cost, they would suffer losses.) But it will often be advantageous for producers to sell *some* of their output at prices less than average cost. A producer can increase its profit any time it can sell one more unit at a price above marginal cost, provided that doing so does not require cutting prices on units sold to other buyers.

The hurdle discount method is an indispensable tool for sellers whose production processes exhibit economies of scale. By making discounts available to price-sensitive buyers without cutting prices to others, it enables them to expand their sales, thus lowering their average cost of production.

Providing airline service between any pair of cities is a production process with economies of scale. Average cost declines with the number of passengers transported. One reason is that the average cost per seat-mile flown is significantly smaller for large aircraft than for small ones. For example, the average cost per seat for a typical domestic flight is 25 percent lower for Boeing's 180-seat 737–900ER than for its 110-seat 737–600. Another factor that makes the cost per available seat-mile smaller on larger aircraft is that that many of the costs of a given flight are fixed, irrespective of the number of passengers carried. Gate costs and the cost of scarce landing and takeoff slots at crowded airports fall into this category. The upshot is that any airline that can attract more passengers to its flights can substantially reduce its average cost of transporting each passenger.

Discount pricing enables sellers to attract more customers. And one of the most effective discount hurdles ever contrived is the Saturday night stay-over requirement for SuperSaver airline fares. As airline marketing executives have long known, business travelers are far less sensitive to airfares than leisure travelers. Business travelers also typically want to spend weekends with their families. Leisure travelers, by contrast, almost always take trips that involve at least one weekend. By making Saturday stay-overs a requisite for SuperSaver discounts, airlines have thus come up with a nearly perfect hurdle: few business travelers are willing to meet this restriction, and most leisure travelers can meet it without effort.

Business travelers often express resentment at paying higher fares than the vacationers in adjacent seats. Yet the airlines' ability to exploit the Saturday stay-over hurdle may create net benefits even for business travelers.

In the air travel market, convenient scheduling is a feature of especially high value to business travelers. But in any city-pair market, the potential traffic volume is limited. So an airline can offer more frequent service economically only if it employs smaller aircraft with higher average cost per seat. Most leisure travelers would be happy to sacrifice the convenience of more frequent service if they could get the lower fares made possible by infrequent flights on larger aircraft.

Because of the Saturday stay-over hurdle, both groups of passengers can do better than if airlines charged the same fares to everyone. By enabling them to attract additional leisure travelers, the restriction permits carriers to employ larger, more efficient aircraft than would otherwise be possible. The resulting cost saving reduces the price premium required to support the frequent service that business travelers demand. At the same time, leisure travelers enjoy the convenience of frequent flights for the same low fares they once had to pay for seats on chartered jumbo jets.

Is it unfair that business travelers pay higher fares because they won't meet the Saturday stay-over requirement? If business travelers did not demand frequent flights, the airlines could employ larger, more efficient aircraft than they currently do. So the higher fares paid by business travelers at least in part reflect the higher costs per seat associated with the smaller aircraft carriers must use to accommodate their demands.

Of course the hurdle discount doesn't apportion the airline's costs with perfect equity. Some leisure travelers demand frequent service, for example, and would be willing to pay for it. They escape having to do so because they can meet the Saturday stay-over requirement. Similarly, some business travelers would be willing to tolerate less frequent service if that meant paying less. On balance, however, there appears to be at least rough justice in the current airline pricing system.

The next examples explore pricing strategies that help producers and consumers share the cost saving from economies of scale.

Why might an appliance retailer hammer dents into the sides of its stoves and refrigerators?

A small fraction of appliances sustain minor cosmetic damage when shipped from manufacturers to retailers. Rather than ship these appliances back to the factory for repairs, retailers discovered that it was simpler to sell them at discount prices. Sears Roebuck was an early champion of the scratch 'n' dent appliance sale.

Drawing by Mick Stevens.

At the annual scratch 'n' dent sale, supplies often run short.

Reports began to circulate, however, that in the days leading up to the sale, Sears had warehouse employees hammering dents into the sides of otherwise unblemished appliances. Were these reports just another urban legend? Or might a profit-seeking retailer have had sound economic reasons for deliberately damaging some of its merchandise?

Again, the goal of any discount scheme is to give a price break to potential customers who wouldn't buy at list price while making the discount available to as few other buyers as possible. Appliance retailers may have discovered by accident that a slightly blemished refrigerator is an excellent hurdle for segregating potential buyers in this way. To participate in a scratch 'n' dent sale, a buyer must clear three hurdles at once. She must take the trouble to find out when the sale occurs; she must clear her calendar so she can get there on that particular day; and she must be prepared to live with the knowledge that her refrigerator has a dent in it, even if the dent will be up against a wall and not visible once the machine is installed. Few high rollers would be willing to jump even one of these hurdles. But as Sears quickly discovered, substantial numbers of price-sensitive shoppers were happy to clear all three.

It is thus by no means far-fetched to imagine that an appliance retailer possessing a limited supply of appliances damaged in transit might find it profitable to send an employee with a hammer out to the warehouse on the day before the annual scratch 'n' dent sale. To the extent the practice expands appliance sales, it reduces the average cost per appliance and thus creates the possibility of lower prices for all consumers.

Why does Apple sell its black laptop computers for $150 more than for otherwise identically configured white ones? *(Chris Frank)*

On July 1, 2006, the Apple website listed the price of the company's thirteen-inch MacBook laptop computer as $1299 for machines with the traditional white plastic case. In contrast, its price for the thirteen-inch MacBook in black was listed at $1499. Close inspection, however, revealed that the black model was equipped with an eighty-gigabyte hard drive, twenty gigabytes larger than the hard drive that was standard in the white model. So far, no mystery: the better machine commanded a higher price. But closer inspection revealed that the white model was also available with an optional eighty-gigabyte hard drive. The surcharge for the bigger drive on the white machine? Just $50. So we have a mystery, after all. Why did the black machine, which costs Apple essentially the same to produce as an identically configured white one, sell for $150 more?

Apple's pricing decision was no doubt influenced by its experience after introducing a black version of its popular iPod in the fall of 2005. Although it was priced the same as the company's traditional white iPod and technically identical to it, demand for black units quickly depleted the company's inventories, even as white ones remained in stock. Because the black version was new, it stood out, causing many more buyers to order it. In setting the same price for the two units, Apple had left cash on the table. By the time it introduced its new MacBook models in the spring of 2006, the company appeared to have learned its lesson. It charged more for the black machines simply because it could.

Is the price premium for black machines unfair? Like the average cost of producing air travel services, the average cost of producing computers declines sharply with the number of units a company produces. This is in large part a consequence of the fact that the company's research and development costs do not vary with the number of units produced. The company can thus add to its profits by selling additional machines at a price below average cost but above its marginal cost. But to underwrite its development costs, the company must also sell some of its units at a price above its average cost.

In a just world, those who care most about the novel features that spring from the company's research and development program would pay a disproportionate share of its cost. Who are those people? Buyers who are least sensitive to price are largely the same ones who would be willing to pay most for the new machine's cutting-edge features. The R&D program benefits all buyers, but it disproportionately benefits those who are willing to pay the most for the new features. The premium price for black machines is a crude device for identifying those buyers. To the extent this hurdle works, buyers of the more expensive black machines have little grounds for complaint.

Why are concerts so much cheaper if you purchase series tickets? *(Michael Li)*

The Chicago Symphony, like most other elite orchestras, sells tickets for individual performances as well as various subscription series. As the name implies, series tickets entitle buyers to attend a group of performances. Such tickets sell at a 35 percent discount from the price of tickets to individual performances. Why are series tickets so much cheaper?

This form of ticket pricing enables the symphony to spread the fixed costs of each performance over larger audiences. Suppose the Chicago Symphony has scheduled a series of two performances. The first consists of music by Berlioz and Tchaikovsky, the second, Bartok and Stravinsky. Let's assume that the potential audience for these performances consists of four groups of equal size. Members of the first group are aficionados of the Romantic period, each of whom would be willing to pay up to $40 for a ticket to the first concert and up to $20 for a ticket to the second. Members of the second group prefer neoclassical music, and would pay up to $20 for the first concert but up to $40 for the second. Members of the third group are passionate Tchaikovsky fans. They would pay up to $45 for the first concert but only up to $5 for the second. Finally, members of the fourth group are passionate fans of Stravinsky. They would pay up to $45 for the second concert but only up to $5 for the first.

Given these assumptions about how potential attendees value the two events, the best the CSO could do if it sold only separate tickets to each event would be to charge $40 for each. At that price, the romantic music lovers and Tchaikovsky fans would attend only the first concert, and the neoclassical music lovers and Stravinsky fans would attend only the second. If there were one hundred members in each of the four groups, the attendance at each event would thus be two hundred, and total ticket revenue would be $16,000.

But now suppose the CSO could offer series tickets for the two events. Its best bet would then be to charge $45 for the individual events ($5 more than before) while selling series tickets for only $30 each ($10 less than before). Under this offering, Tchaikovsky lovers would attend only the first concert and Stravinsky lovers only the second, as before. But whereas the romantic music fans and the neoclassical music fans attended only one concert apiece when tickets were sold only individually, members of these two groups will now attend both concerts. So even though the romantic music fans pay $10 less than before for the first concert, their attendance at the second concert yields a net gain of $20 for the CSO. Similarly, even though the neoclassical music fans pay $10 less than before to attend the second concert, their attendance at the first concert yields another net gain of $20.

Most symphonies struggle to collect enough in ticket revenues each year to defray the costs of their performances. Offering series tickets helps them solve that problem. Again assuming one hundred members in each of the four groups, the CSO would now collect $21,000 in total ticket revenue, or $5,000 more than before. Hence the logic of offering bundled ticket prices.

Why do airlines charge much more for tickets purchased at the last minute, while Broadway theaters follow the opposite practice? *(Gerasimos Efthimiatos)*

Theater fans who go to the TKTS window in New York's Times Square in the afternoon can purchase half-price tickets to many Broadway plays performed the same evening. But someone who books a plane ticket on the same day as the flight can expect to pay a substantial premium, sometimes as much as 100 percent. What explains this difference?

Photo by Jure Marie Sobrito.

*People whose opportunity cost of time is high
are unlikely to stand in line for discounts.*

A seat that is empty when a flight takes off or when the curtain rises means a permanent loss of revenue. Both airlines and theaters face strong incentives to fill as many seats as they can. At the same time, filling a seat at a discount price will often mean losing an opportunity to fill that same seat with someone who would have been willing to pay full list price. So, as always, the marketing challenge is to fill as many seats as possible without taking too big a sacrifice in average revenue per seat.

In the airline industry, marketing executives discovered early on that business travelers are more likely than vacation travelers to change their flight schedules at the last minute. Business travel decisions are also known to be less sensitive to airfare than leisure travel decisions. The airlines' strategy has thus been to charge full price to those who reserve at the last minute (disproportionately business travelers) and give discounts to those who reserve well in advance (mostly leisure travelers).

The balance of forces is slightly different in the theater industry. High-income persons are less sensitive to ticket prices than low-income persons, as in the airline industry, but high-income theatergoers are un-likely to buy tickets at the last minute. Buying half-price tickets at the last minute from the TKTS window confronts theatergoers with two hurdles. One is the need to stand in line, often for an hour or more. Few high-income persons are willing to do that just to save a few dollars. Second and more important, discount tickets are available for only se-lected shows, generally not the most popular ones. High-income per-sons have high opportunity cost of time and are more likely to want to spend a precious free evening watching only the shows they most want to see. Low-income theatergoers, who are much more sensitive to price, find both hurdles much easier to clear. Absent the option of standing in line at TKTS, they might not get to see a Broadway show at all.

Although the specific hurdles are strikingly different in the two cases, both have the effect of filling more seats—and hence of reducing the average cost per customer served—relative to what would have hap-pened in the absence of these hurdles.

Forcing buyers to jump a hurdle in order to become eligible for a discount entails waste to the extent that effort is required to jump the hurdle. But in some cases, the discount hurdle is merely the need to pos-sess a certain piece of information. Once you have it, you pay lower prices thereafter with no additional effort.

If a "cup" is supposed to be eight ounces, why is the smallest cup of coffee listed on the Starbucks menu a "Tall," which contains twelve ounces? (Jennifer Anderson)

Starbucks is the largest purveyor of premium brewed-in-store coffee in the world. Since 1999, the company's menu boards have listed coffee in three sizes: Tall (12 ounces), Grande (16 ounces), and Venti (20 ounces). Yet a cup of coffee is technically only eight ounces and may be as small as six. Even Starbucks's own brewing instructions read, "We recom-mend two tablespoons of ground coffee for each six ounces of water." So why doesn't Starbucks sell a standard cup of coffee?

Actually, it does. If you ask the barista for a "Short," your coffee of choice will be served in the once traditional eight-ounce container. But the Short is nowhere listed on the menu board, and few customers know it's available.

The Short is the company's most discounted cup of coffee. Although a short cappuccino sells for about thirty cents less than the twelve-ounce Tall, it has the same amount of espresso and, because it contains less foamed milk, has a richer taste that many coffee aficionados favor.

The clandestine way Starbucks markets the Short makes this size a form of hurdle price discrimination. The hurdle that prevents customers who are not price-sensitive from buying the discounted Short is that most of them simply don't know about it. In most markets, price-sensitive customers devote more effort than others to sniffing out the best deals. If you were a price-sensitive shopper, the odds are that at least one of your friends would have discovered the Starbucks Short and told you about it. In the meantime, buyers who are less price sensitive will remain content with their twenty-ounce Ventis.

NOT ALL EXAMPLES of price discrimination entail discount hurdles. For instance, when a restaurant offers half-price dinners to patrons over sixty-five, there is no hurdle the thirty-year-old patron can jump to become eligible for the discount. Economists often refer to price differentials of this sort as pure market segmentation, in this case motivated by the fact that senior citizens have lower incomes, on average, than other adults.

Why are round-trip airfares from Kansas City to Orlando lower than round-trip airfares from Orlando to Kansas City? *(Karen Hittle)*

If you lived in Kansas City, Missouri, and wanted to fly to Orlando, Florida, leaving on December 15, 2006, and returning a week later, the lowest round-trip fare you'd have found on Expedia.com would have been $240. But if you lived in Orlando and wanted to fly to Kansas City, the lowest round-trip fare listed for those same dates would have been $312. Passengers on these two itineraries traveled on the same planes consuming the same fuel and enjoyed the same in-flight amenities (or lack thereof). Why, then, were their fares so different?

If you are starting in Kansas City and going to Orlando, you are probably going on vacation. You could go to lots of different places—Hawaii, Barbados, or Cancun, for starters. Because vacationers have many destinations to choose from, airlines must compete fiercely for their business. And given the cost savings inherent in larger aircraft, carriers have a strong incentive to fill additional seats by targeting lower prices to people who are more sensitive to price—vacationers.

But if you are starting in Orlando on a trip to Kansas City, you likely have business or family reasons for traveling. You are probably not shopping for a destination. Buyers with fewer alternatives tend to be less sensitive to price. And that is why travelers originating in Orlando pay more.

THE NEXT EXAMPLES discuss conditions that might motivate sellers to offer free or reduced-price merchandise or product enhancements.

Why do so many restaurants offer free refills on beverages? *(Mike Hedrick)*

The late George Burns once described a business owner who said he lost money on each unit he sold but made it up on volume. Of course, any business that actually followed this practice could not expect to survive for long. The common practice of giving free beverage refills is thus a puzzle. How can restaurants extend this offer and stay in business?

Most businesses sell many goods. To remain afloat, a business need not charge more than the cost of each individual good it sells. Rather, its total revenue must equal or exceed the total cost of goods sold. So if the prices of entrees, desserts, and other items include a sufficient profit margin, a restaurant can offer free refills and still remain in business.

But why would a restaurant *want* to offer free refills? On its face, the practice appears inconsistent with the logic of perfect competition, which holds that people will pay the full cost of any additional goods or services they purchase.

But competition is never perfect. In the restaurant industry, as in many other industries, the average cost per customer served declines with the number of customers served. This means that the average cost of the meals a restaurant serves is higher than the marginal cost of a meal. Because the price a restaurant charges for each meal must be greater than the marginal cost of that meal, any restaurant can increase its profit whenever it can attract additional customers.

Now imagine an initial situation in which no restaurants offered free beverage refills. If a single restaurant were then to extend this offer, what would happen? Diners who ordered beverage refills at that restaurant would feel they were getting a good deal. Word would spread, and in short order this restaurant would find itself serving many more customers than before. Although the restaurant would incur a cost for each additional refill, it would be extremely small.

For the offer to be successful, the restaurant's profit on the extra meals it sells must exceed the cost of the free refills it serves. And since the restaurant's profit margin on the additional meals is likely to be greater than the cost it incurs for each refill, its overall profit should rise.

Seeing the success of this restaurant's free-refill offer, competing restaurants would begin to follow suit, and as more of them did so, the initial restaurant's rise in clientele would diminish. If all restaurants extended the offer, the volume of business at each restaurant would be little different than if none of them offered free refills. And since profit margins in the restaurant industry are traditionally thin, the free-refill offer might seem to portend losses for many restaurants.

Losses might indeed result if the price of meals remained the same throughout this process. But because of the free-refill offer, diners would be receiving more net benefit from the dining experience than before, since they now pay nothing for refills for which they earlier might have had to pay several dollars. The fact that diners are receiving greater net benefit from their dining experience enables restaurants to raise their meal prices. When the dust settles, meal prices can be expected to have increased by roughly the small amount necessary to cover the cost of the free refills.

Another factor to consider is that restaurants typically charge $2 or so for a few cents worth of iced tea or soft drink syrup and carbonated water. For the extra costs to matter, someone would have to drink a prodigious number of refills. If just 10 percent of customers ordered a beverage instead of water because of the free-refill offer, the restaurant would be almost certain to come out ahead. This reasoning suggests that restaurants that serve soft drinks and iced tea in cans should be less likely than others to offer free refills, which is in fact the case. Again, the exception that proves the rule.

Why do VCRs have so many features when the average person doesn't use a majority of the features found on even the simplest machines? *(Deborah Bair)*

The typical purchaser of a video cassette recorder wants a machine that will enable the family to watch movies or record its favorite television programs. All models currently on sale have these capabilities. But they also have a bewildering list of additional capabilities that most consumers never use. Many machines, for example, automatically place a signal on the videotape control at the beginning of each individually recorded program, which enables the user to "access each program by pressing the corresponding 1–9 keys via remote." And most models now offer on-screen programming instructions in English, Spanish, or French. Although many of these features are undeniably useful, some buyers complain that the machines are so complicated that they have difficulty using them. Why don't manufacturers make cheaper and simpler machines available to these buyers?

Although some buyers do not value having additional technical capabilities on their VCRs, many others do. Manufacturers add such features in an effort to compete more effectively for customers in the latter group. Most of the costs of adding a new feature are fixed research and development costs. Once these are incurred, the marginal cost of adding the feature to a machine is typically small.

It would be possible, of course, for manufacturers to offer scores of different machines, each with a different level of technical capability. But most retailers have little interest in stocking such a large number of machines. In any event, since the marginal cost of producing the simplest machine would hardly be less than for the most advanced one, consumers would save little by buying the simplest machine. So manufacturers have chosen to offer advanced technical features on almost all the machines they produce.

Consumers yearning for a simpler machine will have to hope that manufacturers will soon add yet another feature, a button that disables, or at least hides, all but the most basic features.

Why do budget airlines charge for onboard meals (which are typically free on luxury airlines), while luxury hotels charge for Internet access (which is typically free at budget hotels)? *(Jia Dai)*

Free in-flight meals, once the norm on almost all airlines, are now regularly offered only on premium-price carriers, such as Singapore Airlines. Travelers who fly United or American are now expected to either bring their own food onboard or purchase boxed meals in flight. In contrast, luxury hotels like the Four Seasons typically charge $10 or more a day for in-room Internet access, while budget hotels like the Hampton Inn routinely offer the same service free of charge. Why this difference?

In a perfectly competitive market, the no cash on the table principle suggests that customers who opt for additional services can expect to pay extra for them. The logic is that if a company tried to offer an additional service for "free" by including it in the price of the basic product, a rival seller could lure away customers who didn't want that service by setting a lower price for the basic product and charging separately for the service.

In practice, of course, no market is perfectly competitive. But the market for seats on budget airlines is closer to being perfectly competitive than the market for seats on luxury airlines. The latter are fewer in number and offer more specialized services. For similar reasons, the market for rooms in budget hotels is closer to being perfectly competitive than the market for rooms in luxury hotels. These observations seem to suggest that additional services would be more likely to be priced separately in both budget hotels and budget airlines. So the no cash on the table principle can explain why budget airlines charge for meals while luxury airlines include them in the base price. It can also explain why most airlines might have offered meals for free in the past, since the entire air travel market was a luxury market until relatively recently. But the no cash on the table principle appears, at first glance, incompatible with the opposite pricing pattern we observe for Internet access in hotels.

A plausible conjecture is that the reversal is rooted in a difference in the cost structures for providing these two services. The cost of catered meal service goes up in rough proportion to the number of meals served. But the cost of providing Internet access is largely fixed. Once a hotel has installed a wireless Internet network, the marginal cost of allowing another guest to log on is literally zero.

The no cash on the table principle tells us that the more competitive a market for a good or service is, the closer its price will be to marginal cost. So if the market for budget hotel rooms is indeed more competitive than the market for luxury hotel rooms, it follows that Internet access is more likely to be included in the room price at budget hotels. Budget hotels might like to charge extra for Internet access, but since the marginal cost of providing access is zero, some budget hotel would be sure to advertise free Internet access. Price-sensitive travelers would be attracted by that offer, forcing other budget hotels to follow suit. Budget airlines are not under similar pressure to offer free meal services because the marginal cost of each meal served is positive.

Luxury hotels may charge for Internet access because their clientele tends to be either independently wealthy or traveling on expense account, and hence not highly sensitive to price. Still, if enough guests begin complaining about the practice, the fact that the marginal cost of providing Internet access is zero suggests that some luxury hotels may start including access in their room rates. If that happens, other luxury hotels will be under pressure to follow suit.

IN THE NEXT TWO EXAMPLES sellers appear to have the power to either charge higher prices or impose cancellation penalties, yet for strategic reasons they choose not to exercise that power.

Why do many amusement parks not charge extra for their most popular rides, even though there are always long waiting lines for them?

As of January 1, 2006, Disney World in Orlando, Florida, charged $55.16 for a children's day pass providing unlimited free access to the park's rides. More precisely, access is unlimited only in a limited sense: children can go on any ride as often as they wish, but for the most popular rides, there is almost always a long line. During the busiest periods, for example, a ride on Space Mountain, the park's most popular attraction, can entail a wait of more than an hour. Why doesn't Disney impose a surcharge for its most popular rides?

By themselves, waiting lines are not necessarily evidence that sellers are leaving cash on the table. For example, the number of patrons who wish to dine at a restaurant on a given evening is highly variable, making it hard to set prices at levels that will exactly fill the seats every evening with no waiting. What economists generally do not expect to see, however, are persistent, predictable waiting lines like the ones at Disney World.

One possible explanation is suggested by the fact that it is parents, not children, who pay for trips to Disney World. Imagine how a day at the park might play out if the additional charge per ride for Space Mountain were set at whatever level would eliminate waiting lines—say, $10 a ride. Many children would still want to ride Space Mountain continuously, and now it would be possible for them to do so. Before long, most parents would be forced to say no, not just once but repeatedly. Can anyone imagine a family leaving the park with pleasant memories?

By charging a flat fee and using queues to ration access to its most popular rides, Disney's management may have struck the most reasonable compromise available.

Why do rental car companies impose no penalty for canceling a reservation at the last minute, whereas both hotels and airlines impose significant cancellation charges?

If you buy a ticket to the theater and then miss the performance because you got stuck in traffic, you don't get a refund. It is the same with some airline tickets. If you don't show up for your flight, your ticket becomes worthless. At the very least, the airline will charge you a stiff cancellation fee. Similarly, most hotels will charge you for your room if you cancel your reservation after 6:00 P.M. on the day you're supposed to arrive. But rental car companies follow a completely different practice. You need not provide your credit card number when you reserve a rental car.

And if you don't show up to claim the car you reserved, there is no financial penalty at all. Why this difference?

Car rental companies, like all other sellers, want to keep their customers happy. Customers don't like cancellation fees, and a rental car company that does not charge them would have a competitive advantage over other companies that did. Airlines and hotels, of course, have the same motive to avoid cancellation fees. Presumably they charge such fees because allowing customers to cancel without penalty at the last minute would also be costly. Airlines would have many more unfilled seats on each flight, and hotels would have many more empty rooms. It each case, it would be necessary to charge substantially higher prices to stay in business.

In principle, rental car companies should face the same pressure. Their failure to impose cancellation fees may be rooted in the fact that their typical customer's transaction happens to be immediately preceded by an airline transaction and immediately followed by a hotel transaction. Because both hotels and airlines impose cancellation fees, the typical rental car customer has a strong incentive to show up for his car at the assigned time, even in the absence of rental car cancellation fees. Rental car companies may thus be able to avoid alienating customers who are forced to cancel because the cancellation policies of hotels and airlines ensure that there will be few such customers.

5

Arms Races and the Tragedy of the Commons

A dam Smith's invisible hand is one of the most celebrated ideas in economics. Smith was the first to see clearly how the pursuit of individual self-interest in the marketplace often promotes the greatest good for all. For example, producers adopt cost-saving innovations hoping to earn higher profits, only to discover that when rival firms follow suit, the ultimate benefits accrue to consumers in the form of lower prices.

Unlike many economists today who celebrate the invisible hand, Smith harbored no illusion that unbridled competition *always* produces the greatest good for all. In *The Wealth of Nations*, for example, he advances a more limited claim about the consequences of self-interested behavior on the part of a business owner: "By pursuing his own interest, he *frequently* promotes that of the society more effectually than when he really intends to promote it." (Emphasis added.)

It fell to Charles Darwin—the father of evolutionary biology and a man strongly influenced by the writings of Adam Smith, Thomas Malthus, and other economists—to identify a deep and wide-ranging conflict between individual and group interests. Darwin's central claim

Photo by Duke Conrad.

Big antlers: Smart for one, dumb for all?

was that natural selection favors traits and behaviors that increase individual reproductive success. Whether they serve any positive purpose for the species as a whole is largely beside the point. Some traits, such as intelligence, not only contribute to individual reproductive success but also serve the broader interests of the species. Other traits serve individual interests only to harm the larger group. The prodigious antlers of male elk are a clear illustration of the latter.

Like bull elephant seals and males in most other polygynous species, male elk battle one another for access to females. Their antlers are their principal weapons in these battles, and an elk with larger antlers than its rival is more likely to prevail. So elk with bigger antlers win more mates, causing their antler genes to appear in the next generation with higher frequency. Antlers thus became the focus of a runaway evolutionary arms race.

Although big antlers help gain access to females, they also make it harder to escape from wolves and other predators in densely wooded ar-

Photo by Christian Boice.

The contest for mates: The ultimate winner-take-all tournament?

eas. Elk would thus have good reasons to prefer that each animal's rack of antlers be reduced by half. After all, it is relative antler size that counts in battle. So if all males had smaller antlers, each fight would be resolved as before, yet each animal would enjoy increased security from predators.

Natural selection, which is the source of the problem, cannot be its solution. True, a mutant elk with smaller antlers would enjoy relative immunity from predators. But he wouldn't command access to a harem. So copies of his genes wouldn't make it into the next generation, which is the only payoff that matters in the Darwinian framework.

Oversize antlers belong to a class of traits that we may call smart for one, dumb for all. Examples abound in everyday life. The cost-benefit principle suggests that individuals will take actions when personal benefits exceed personal costs. If the individual decision maker reaps all the benefits and bears all the costs associated with an action, we get Adam Smith's invisible hand. But many individual actions generate benefits or costs that accrue to others.

When some in an audience stand to get a better view, for example, they block the sight lines of those behind them. Similarly, when additional fishing boats set sail, they reduce the amount of fish caught by existing boats. In such cases the invisible hand tends to break down. All stand to get a better view, yet none sees better than if all had remained seated. And if fishermen set sail whenever the net value of what they expect to catch exceeds their opportunity cost of time and other expenses, the result is overfishing, a "tragedy of the commons."

In this chapter, we will see that divergence between individual and social interests helps us answer a host of fascinating questions.

Why do physicians tend to overprescribe antibiotics? *(Fred Heberle)*

When patients complain of minor ear and respiratory infections, many doctors prescribe antibiotics. If the infection was caused by bacteria (as opposed to viruses), antibiotic treatment is likely to speed recovery. But each time a patient takes antibiotics, there is a small risk that a drug-resistant strain of bacteria will emerge. Public health officials therefore urge physicians to prescribe antibiotics only in response to serious infections. Why do so many physicians continue to prescribe them for minor ones?

Most physicians understand that drug resistance emerges quickly and reliably when antibiotics are widely prescribed. A strain of staphylococcus bacterium (*Staphylococcus aureus*), for example, was discovered to be resistant to penicillin in 1947, just four years after the antibiotic entered widespread use. Most physicians also know that antibiotic-resistant strains can cause serious trouble. Once *Staphylococcus aureus* emerged, physicians started treating it with another antibiotic, methicillin, but that strategy worked only temporarily. Methicillin-resistant bacteria (MRSA) were first discovered in the United Kingdom in 1961 and are now common in hospitals everywhere. MRSA infections were responsible for 37 percent of fatal cases of blood poisoning in the United Kingdom in 1999, up from only 4 percent in 1991.

Overprescription of antibiotics is a tragedy of the commons, much like the overharvesting of fish in the oceans. Just as the amount of fish caught by an individual fisherman cannot by itself cause a fish population to crash, no single prescription of antibiotics can produce lethal drug-resistant bacteria. Yet each time an antibiotic is prescribed, at least some of the bacteria that caused the patient's infection tend to survive.

Individual bacterial cells in the colony are all different, and the ones most likely to survive a course of antibiotic treatment are unfortunately not a random sample of the original colony. Rather, their genetic structure was least vulnerable to the drug. These survivors may still be susceptible to higher doses, but as additional mutations accumulate over time, drug resistance in the surviving bacteria becomes more powerful.

The dilemma confronting doctors is that patients demand antibiotics in the belief that taking them will hasten their recovery. Some physicians refuse to treat minor infections in this way but others give in, knowing that their patients may seek other doctors if they do not. The Centers for Disease Control estimates that roughly one-third of the 150 million antibiotic prescriptions written each year are unnecessary.

Acceding to patient requests is probably made easier by the knowledge that no single prescription will cause the emergence of a drug-resistant strain. Unfortunately, the aggregate effect is that such decisions virtually guarantee more virulent strains.

Why do women endure the discomfort of high heels? *(Digby Lock)*

High heels are uncomfortable and make walking more difficult. Prolonged use can injure the feet, knees, and back. Why do women keep wearing them?

The short answer seems to be that women in heels are more likely to attract favorable notice. In *Sense and Sensibility*, Jane Austen describes the character Elinor Dashwood as having a "delicate complexion, regular features, and. . . remarkably pretty figure." But Austen describes Elinor's sister Marianne as "still handsomer. Her form, though not so correct as her sister's, in having the advantage of height, was more striking." In addition to making women taller, high heels force the back to arch, pushing the bosom forward and the buttocks rearward, thus accentuating the female form. "Men like an exaggerated female figure," writes fashion historian Caroline Cox.

The problem is that if all women wear high heels, such advantages tend to cancel out. Height, after all, is a relative phenomenon. It may be advantageous to be several inches taller than others, or at least not to be several inches shorter. But when all wear shoes that make them several

Drawing by Mick Stevens.

In dating as in sports, height is often advantageous.

inches taller, the relative height distribution is unaffected, so no one appears taller than if all had worn flat heels. If women could decide collectively what kind of shoes to wear, all might agree to forgo high heels. But because any individual can gain advantage by wearing them, such an agreement might be hard to maintain.

Why do so many supermarkets, even those in small towns, stay open twenty-four hours a day?

Ithaca, a town of about 30,000 in upstate New York, has five all-night grocery stores. Shoppers who visit one at 4:00 A.M. will almost invariably find themselves the only nonemployees in the store. The costs of keeping a store open all night are not huge, but neither are they insignificant.

Heating, air-conditioning, and lighting bills, for example, are higher than if stores were to close between midnight and 6:00 A.M. Night shift cashiers, stock clerks, and security personnel must also be paid premium wages. Since these costs almost certainly exceed the additional profits from sales in wee hours, why do these stores stay open all night?

The factors that influence consumers' decisions about where to shop for groceries include price, variety, location, and hours. Most consumers will pick the store that best meets their preferences and then do most of their shopping there. Once you learn the layout in one store, why spend time trying to find things in another? Stores thus face strong incentives to become the first choice of as many consumers as possible.

The prices and variety of goods stocked tend to vary little from store to store, but where those factors differ, they may be decisive for some shoppers. People probably won't shop regularly at a store that is well out of their way, but location is not likely to be crucial for small-town residents who own cars. Now suppose that all supermarkets close between 11:00 P.M. and 7:00 A.M. If one store extended its closing time until midnight, it would become the store with the most convenient hours. Even consumers who would shop between 11:00 and midnight only on rare occasions would thus have a reason for choosing it as their regular store: the ability to find things easily whenever late-night shopping needs arose. Although a supermarket might attract only a few shoppers during the extra hour between 11:00 and midnight, maintaining its convenient hours would induce more shoppers to choose it as their regular store.

Rather than see their regular customers desert them, rival supermarkets would have a powerful incentive to match the extended hours. But then some other stores could gain ground by moving their closing time back to 1:00 A.M. If the costs of keeping largely empty stores open an additional hour are not too great, the only stable outcome could be for most major stores to remain open all night. And that, apparently, is what happened in Ithaca.

Given that most supermarkets stay open all night in Ithaca, a newcomer's choice among them no longer depends on their hours. So supermarkets continue to compete on other dimensions. One is known for having the best baked goods, for example, another for having the best selection of international ingredients. But none seems poised to start closing at night again.

Grocery stores did not always stay open all night in Ithaca, and there are cities of similar size with no all-night stores. So although the competitive dynamics described above seem a plausible account of why stores stay open all night in Ithaca, they clearly do not explain the timing or geographic diffusion of this development.

Why do retailers put Christmas decorations on display in September?
(Melissa Moore, Eric Sass)

Although the holiday shopping season does not "officially" begin until the Friday after Thanksgiving, artificial trees and holiday wreaths now appear in some stores as early as September. These earlier displays entail opportunity costs, since shelves used for holiday merchandise cannot be used to display other merchandise. So early holiday displays come at the expense of reduced sales of other merchandise. Since the total amount of money that shoppers spend on holiday merchandise is largely independent of the length of the holiday season, why are merchants putting this merchandise on display so early?

The holiday season accounts for approximately 40 percent of annual retail sales volume and almost 65 percent of annual retail profits. If most merchants waited until the Friday after Thanksgiving before putting Christmas wreaths on display, any individual merchant could gain advantage by putting them on display earlier—say, the Friday before Thanksgiving. This would not increase the total number of wreaths sold, but it would take sales away from other merchants.

In self-defense, other merchants would put their holiday merchandise on display earlier, too, and the stage would then be set for the start date to move still earlier. As the retail marketplace has grown more competitive in recent years, the unofficial start date for putting holiday merchandise on display is now right after Labor Day in many markets.

Will we eventually see year-round displays of holiday merchandise—much as we saw with twenty-four-hour supermarkets? It's possible but not likely. Supermarkets remain open all night because the cost of staying open an additional hour is fairly small. But using shelf space for holiday merchandise means not being able to use it for other merchandise, and beyond some point that opportunity cost looms large. Retailers who cannot find more profitable uses for their limited shelf space than to display holiday merchandise in March are unlikely to survive for long.

Why do cherries that grow on trees in public parks get eaten "too soon"?

Cherries, like all fruit, go through a natural ripening cycle. In the early stages they are too tart to eat, but as the cycle progresses, the sugar content of the fruit increases, making them more appealing to most palates. Professional cherry growers time their harvests so that the fruit appears in supermarkets near the apex of the ripening cycle. Invariably, however, cherries on trees growing in public parks are picked when they are barely sweet enough to be edible. If people left them on the tree a little longer, they would be much more pleasing. Why don't people wait?

Professional cherry growers plant their trees on private land, and trespassers who pick cherries from them are subject to legal sanctions. These growers have no incentive to harvest their fruit prematurely. After all, grocers will pay them more for ripe fruit because consumers are willing to pay higher prices for it.

But the incentives are different in public parks, where anyone is at liberty to pick cherries. And although everyone would be better off if the fruit were allowed to ripen, anyone who waited that long would find no cherries to pick.

Cherries growing in public parks begin to disappear the moment they become just ripe enough that eating them is better than nothing. At that stage, they don't deliver much pleasure. But because others can't be prevented from picking them, there's little hope of finding any ripe ones.

Why does the practice of check splitting cause people to spend more at restaurants?

Friends who dine together at restaurants commonly split the check evenly. This practice is easier for the service staff than preparing a separate check for each diner. It is also much easier than trying to keep track of who ordered what and adjusting everyone's contribution accordingly. Still, many find the practice objectionable because those who order inexpensively are forced to pay more than the actual cost of what they ate and drank. But there is another objectionable consequence of check splitting: it gives everyone an incentive to spend more than if each were paying separately. Why does check splitting have this effect?

Consider a group of ten friends who have agreed in advance to split their restaurant check equally. And suppose a member of the group has narrowed his choice to the regular serving of prime rib of beef, with a menu price of $20, and a large portion for $30. Assume further that the additional benefit from the large portion is worth $5 more to him than the smaller one. If he were eating by himself, he would order the regular serving because the $5 of additional benefit from the large portion is less than its $10 extra cost. But because the group has agreed to split the check evenly, ordering the larger portion will make his share of the total bill go up by only $1 (his one-tenth share of the extra $10 for the larger portion). And since the larger portion is worth $5 extra to him, he will order it.

Economists call such decisions inefficient because the $4 net gain to the person from ordering the larger portion (the additional $5 by which he values that portion minus the $1 extra he ends up having to contribute) is smaller than the net loss imposed on the rest of the group (the $9 increase in the total amount they pay because their friend ordered the large portion).

Although check splitting can be both unfair and inefficient, the practice is unlikely to disappear. The losses involved are usually small, after all, and the practice does make the transaction more convenient.

Why does an accident in the northbound lanes of a divided highway cause a traffic jam in the southbound lanes? *(Thomas Schelling)*

When an accident occurs in the northbound lanes of an expressway, it is easy to see why traffic gets backed up in those lanes. The damaged cars, ambulances, and police cars often make the northbound lanes impassable for hours. But why should the accident cause traffic to back up—often for miles—in the southbound lanes?

Drawing by Mick Stevens.

The rubbernecker's curiosity: Is the delay worth it?

As they approach the scene of the accident, southbound drivers make a simple cost-benefit calculation. The cost of slowing down to take a closer look at the accident scene is that they will be delayed by several seconds. The benefit is that by so doing, they will satisfy their curiosity. To judge from their behavior, the benefit seems to exceed the cost for most motorists. What most motorists do not consider, of course, is that one's decision to slow down for several seconds also creates several seconds of delay for each of the hundreds or thousands of motorists behind. So the aggregate cost of getting a better look at the accident might be a delay of more than an hour per motorist.

It seems unlikely that many motorists would be willing to endure an hour's delay to get a better look at an accident scene. If motorists could take a binding vote on the matter, they would almost surely elect not to slow down. But they make their decisions on this matter one by one when they reach the spot of the accident. At that point, having already paid the cost of curiosity, most motorists—even those in a hurry—choose to slow down.

THE FINAL EXAMPLES in this chapter illustrate that when individual and group interests fail to coincide, people can take a variety of steps to reconcile them.

Why do hockey players vote unanimously for rules that require helmets, even though, when left to their own devices, they almost invariably skate without them? (Thomas Schelling)

By skating without a helmet, a player increases his team's odds of winning, perhaps because he can see and hear a little better or more effectively intimidate opponents. The downside is that he also increases his odds of injury. If he values the higher odds of winning more than he values the extra safety, he will discard his helmet. Yet when others inevitably follow suit, the competitive balance is restored—everyone faces more risk and no one benefits. Hence the attraction of helmet rules.

Why do many schools require students to wear school uniforms?

Many people consider the freedom to dress as they please a fundamental right. Yet when they become parents of school-age children, many of these same people become sympathetic to schools that require students to wear uniforms. Why would schools enact such requirements and why would so many parents support them?

When students are free to choose what clothes they wear, they must consider the implicit messages about themselves they send to others. Someone who wishes to convey that she is bold, for example, might wear clothing that is conspicuously daring. Someone who wishes to appear successful and in command might want to wear clothing of conspicuously high quality. But terms like "daring" and "quality" are inherently relative. If many students begin to wear clothing that stands out with respect to the norms that define these qualities, the norms themselves will shift. As with the antlers on male elk, a costly arms race can ensue.

The obvious downside of requiring school uniforms is to limit students' ability to express themselves. The upside is that they reduce the costs, both monetary and emotional, of clothing arms races.

Why have many high schools abandoned the practice of naming a valedictorian?

At most high school graduation ceremonies, the closing address was traditionally given by the class valedictorian—usually the student with the highest overall grade point average. In recent years, however, many high schools have abandoned the practice of naming a valedictorian. What motivated them to take this step?

Competition for admission to elite universities has intensified. New York University, for example, recently accepted only one of every fourteen applicants. In this climate high school students are under more pressure than ever to assemble impressive academic records. And because few credentials are more impressive than being named the valedictorian of your graduating class, competition for that honor has also intensified. Administrators at many schools decided that the race to become valedictorian had taken on disproportionate importance in the lives of top students, many of whom were sacrificing important life experiences in the hope of earning the highest possible grades in every course. By discontinuing the practice of naming a valedictorian, these administrators hoped to defuse a costly positional arms race.

Why do bureaucrats favor the passive voice? *(Alfred Kahn)*

Alfred Kahn, a former economics professor at Cornell University, was tapped in 1977 by President Jimmy Carter to become chairman of the Civil Aeronautics Board. The CAB, now defunct, was the federal agency that regulated fares and routes in the civil aviation industry. Kahn's charge was to deregulate that industry and put the agency out of business.

On arriving in Washington, he was surprised to discover that most of the regulatory orders issued by the CAB's legal staff were almost incomprehensible. Passages like these were common:

> The holder [of a CAB certificate] may continue to serve regularly any point named herein through the airport last regularly used by the holder to serve such point prior to the effective date of the certificate. Upon compliance with such procedures relating thereto as may be prescribed by the Board, the holder may, in addition to the services hereinabove expressly prescribed, regularly serve a point named herein through any airport convenient thereto.

Kahn's first memo to his legal staff announced that he would reject any document that was not written in plain English. "Read your documents to your spouses and children," he told them, "and if they laugh, you need to rewrite." But why were these documents so difficult to understand in the first place?

A regulator's task is to regulate people. This generally entails telling them they cannot do what they want. Most people do not take pleasure in frustrating the wishes of others. It is understandable that bureaucrats might wish to downplay their own roles in the process. Rather than say, "I forbid United Airlines to fly between San Diego and San Antonio," for example, regulators might find it more comfortable to say something like, "It has been determined not to be in the public interest that United Airlines continue to provide air transportation services between San Diego and San Antonio."

Kahn's edict was widely publicized at the time and drew worldwide applause from fans of clear language. In its wake CAB documents quickly became clearer and more concise.

Did the new mode of communication persist? With most CAB lawyers having long since dispersed to other jobs, no one really knows. But there is reason to suspect that the plain-English mode is not a stable equilibrium among bureaucrats. If plain English became the norm, it would then be in the interests of any one bureaucrat to move ever so slightly in the direction of vagueness, thereby to diminish the visibility of his or her responsibility for restricting other people's behavior. Too big a shift would risk a reprimand, but a slight shift would attract little notice. As other bureaucrats then responded to the same incentive, the standards of vagueness would begin to shift. It is easy to see how, through a gradual, step-by-step process, the result might again be thoroughly unintelligible bureaucratic language. Such language probably would persist until another forceful leader emerged to demand greater clarity.

6

The Myth of Ownership

Peole who grow up in modern Western industrial countries often take for granted the idea that if you own something, you are free to do as you please with it. And within reasonably broad limits, that understanding serves well enough. For example, owning a bicycle in most countries entails the right to use it anytime you please, to tell others they cannot use it, and to sell it to whomever you choose.

That living standards in the United States and many other industrialized nations have risen more than forty-fold since the late eighteenth century owes much to well-defined and strongly enforced systems of property rights. In contrast, societies that lack such systems seldom become wealthy. If people cannot establish clear legal title to property, they have little incentive to invest in the capital equipment that generates new wealth.

But while property rights create enormous benefits, they also entail costs. To define and enforce property rights for any particular good requires the expenditure of real resources. Sometimes the resulting benefits are not worth it. On closer inspection it becomes clear that the concept of ownership is in fact highly contested. This chapter begins with examples that probe the limits of our understanding of what it means to own something.

Why is it sometimes illegal for an island homeowner to prevent strangers from using his dock?

On November 13, 1904, several members of the Ploof family were sailing on Lake Champlain when a storm broke. Seeking shelter, they moored their sloop at a dock owned by a man named Putnam, who lived in a house on an island in the lake. Putnam sent a servant to order the Ploofs to cast off from the dock. They did so, and soon their sloop capsized in the storm. Several family members were injured but all survived. The Ploofs later filed suit against Putnam, and a Vermont court found in their favor in 1908. Why was it illegal for Putnam to prevent the Ploofs from using his dock?

The laws of private property grant owners considerable, but not absolute, power to decide how their property is used. The Vermont court found that the cost of denying the Ploofs refuge from the storm outweighed any benefit Putnam might have gained by exercising complete control over his dock.

Why is the law of trespass often suspended along waterfront property?

City dwellers do not have the legal right to walk across someone else's property just because doing so will speed their arrival at their intended destination. They must use sidewalks and other public rights of way to get where they are going. In many jurisdictions, however, lakefront and oceanfront properties are governed by different rules. For example, if people living in a lakefront cottage want to visit friends living three cottages to the north, they are legally entitled to walk directly across the two intervening properties, no matter how strenuously the owners of those properties might object. Why this difference?

Like all other laws, laws against trespass entail costs and benefits. Since homeowners generally value privacy and security, they gain when others are prevented from trespassing on their land. In the process, some are prevented from choosing the most convenient routes to their destinations. The magnitudes of these costs and benefits are different in different contexts.

The benefits of trespass are lower in city nieghborhoods (left)
than along waterfront property (right).

Suppose the owner of the house at A in the city neighborhood in the accompanying drawing wants to visit a friend who lives in the house at D. He could shorten his walk by cutting through the yards of the houses at B and C. If he were prevented from trespassing on those properties, the length of his walk would increase, but not by much, since there are public rights of way close at hand. Under these circumstances, the value of privacy trumps the value of a shorter route.

But now suppose the houses in question are located along a lakeshore, as in the lower right portion of the drawing. If the person who lives in the house at A wants to visit her friend who lives in the house at D, it will be just a short walk if she is permitted to cross the property of the people who own houses at B and C. But if forced to use public rights of way, she will have to ascend a steep driveway of perhaps half a mile or more in length, then drive north for a similar distance before finally descending another difficult driveway. In many cases, the costs of such trajectories would justify waiving the law of trespass along waterfront property.

But this cannot be the entire explanation, since waterfront properties are exempt from trespass laws even when roads run close to the shoreline and apply inland even when roads are far away. The exemption for waterfront property may stem also from the fact that bodies of water have historically been common property, open to all. This openness would be meaningless without a corresponding right of access. In times when more people fished, the right of access was economically important. In places like Maine, it still is, and newcomers who try to restrict the use of their beaches generate local controversy.

Why did Native Americans living in the Pacific Northwest define and enforce private property rights in land, while those living on the Great Plains did not?

The most important economic resources for Native Americans living on the Great Plains were the herds of wild buffalo that inhabited the region. Because buffalo congregate in large groups that roam for hundreds of miles, enforcing private rights to buffalo grazing land would have meant partitioning the Great Plains and building thousands of miles of costly fencing. Because the herds were so large relative to the number of animals that hunters killed each year, the benefit of enforcing such rights did not justify the costs.

In contrast, Native Americans living in the Northwest Territories earned their living primarily by trapping small animals for meat and fur. These animals typically did not roam over great distances but spent their entire lives on small parcels of land. Defining property rights to the land that individual Native American families lived on was tantamount to conferring trapping rights to the specific animals that inhabited those same parcels. The cost-benefit principle thus suggests a parsimonious explanation for why the two groups of Native Americans followed such different approaches to property rights.

Why does the law grant ownership of a piece of land to someone who has occupied it illegally for at least ten years? *(Plana Lee)*

In New York State, someone who has occupied the same piece of property continuously for a period of ten years is entitled to claim legal ownership of it, even though someone else might have originally paid for it. Why does the law reward trespassers in this way?

Variations of this law have been described as squatters rights, or laws of adverse possession. They have a simple economic rationale—the interests of the community are not well served by allowing valuable property to sit unused. Owners of potentially valuable property sometimes disappear without a trace, leaving no heirs. Others ignore their property for extended periods. By granting squatters rights, the law encourages owners to either make good use of their property or else sell it. By establishing waiting periods of ten years or longer, adverse possession laws pose little threat to the interests of legitimate property owners. After all, property left untended for extended periods must be of little economic value to those who hold title to it.

THE DIFFICULTY OF ENFORCING property rights can help us understand why resources are managed more efficiently in some cases than in others.

Why are whales in danger of extinction, but not chickens?

Seldom does a year pass without a street demonstration by environmental activists decrying international hunting that threatens extinction for many large marine mammal species. Yet to my knowledge there has never been a demonstration exhorting us to save chickens. Why not?

The short answer is that chickens have never been an endangered species. But that just begs the question of why one species is endangered and another not.

Whale populations have been dwindling because no one owns whales. They swim in international waters, and several nations have refused to respect the international treaties that have attempted to protect them.

Drawing by Mick Stevens.

Whales and buffalo: Something in common?

Japanese and Norwegian whalers understand perfectly well that their current practices threaten the survival of whales and hence their own livelihood. But each whaler also knows that any whale he does not harvest will be taken by someone else. Thus no whaler stands to gain from self-restraint.

In contrast, most chickens in the world are owned by someone. If you kill one of your chickens today, that is one less chicken you will own tomorrow. If chicken farming were your livelihood, you would have strong incentives to balance the number of birds you send to market and the number of new chicks you acquire.

Chickens and whales are both economically valuable. The fact that people enjoy secure property rights in chickens but not in whales explains why the former are secure and the latter are endangered.

Why is pollution a more serious problem in the Mediterranean Sea than in the Great Salt Lake?

Many countries that border the Mediterranean Sea dump raw sewage and a host of other pollutants into it. In contrast, the Great Salt Lake is remarkably free of pollution. What explains this difference?

Some might argue that the Great Salt Lake is cleaner because the Mormon culture is more respectful of nature than the secular cultures of the countries that surround the Mediterranean. Perhaps so, but a more economically compelling explanation is that whereas the Great Salt Lake lies entirely within the borders of a single political jurisdiction (the state of Utah), more than two dozen sovereign nations surround the Mediterranean. If Utah enacts regulations limiting toxic discharge into the Great Salt Lake, its citizens bear the cost of those regulations, but they also receive 100 percent of the benefit. In contrast, if an individual Mediterranean nation enacted similar regulations, its citizens would bear their full cost but would reap only a small fraction of the resulting benefit, most of which would accrue to the citizens of other nations. The disparity gives each Mediterranean nation an incentive to rely on the cleanup efforts of other nations, a problem that does not exist in the case of the Great Salt Lake.

Why did the fall of the former Soviet Union spell gloom for aficionados of Caspian Sea caviar? *(Thomas Gellert)*

For gourmets around the globe, there is no greater delicacy than caviar from the Caspian Sea. The rarest and most precious variety comes from the Beluga sturgeon, which can grow up to 30 feet long, weigh as much as 1,800 pounds, and live as long as 100 years. Beluga caviar has long been expensive but readily available. Since the dissolution of the former Soviet Union in 1989, however, supplies have plummeted, and its price has escalated sharply. What went wrong?

The Caspian Sea is now surrounded by Iran and four independent nations that were once part of the Soviet Union: Russia, Kazakhstan, Turkmenistan, and Azerbaijan. Before 1989, the powerful central governments of Iran and the Soviet Union tightly regulated commercial activity in the Caspian Sea. They kept the tragedy of the commons under control by prohibiting the harvest of smaller sturgeon. When the Soviet Union's demise left central governments unable to maintain strict regulatory control, sturgeon fishermen realized that restraint was no longer economically viable. Any sturgeon they left behind would simply have been harvested by others.

Russia and Iran have again begun cooperating in an effort to curb pollution and overfishing in the Caspian Sea. In the meantime, however, buyers can expect to continue paying more than $160 an ounce for Beluga caviar.

The law not only affects what people are allowed to do with their property but also influences how social institutions evolve. In particular, it helps explain why some institutions are organized as private, for-profit firms, others as nonprofits, and still others as publicly funded ones.

Why aren't there any top-ranked for-profit universities? *(Ashees Jain)*

Among the hundreds of top-ranked universities in the United States, not one is a for-profit institution. Most other institutions of higher education are also nonprofit. The most conspicuous exceptions are for-profit institutions (such as the University of Phoenix) that specialize in vocational instruction and disavow any aim of achieving elite academic status. Why are schools at the top of the educational hierarchy exclusively nonprofit?

Top-ranked universities in the United States often cover only one-third or less of their expenses out of tuition revenues. The remainder comes mostly from gifts—either cash grants from current alumni or the interest from endowments funded mostly by current and past alumni. On the assumption that few alumni would make donations to universities organized as for-profit institutions, nonprofit universities thus enjoy an obvious competitive advantage.

But nonprofit institutions would enjoy an edge even in the absence of accumulated endowments. Suppose, plausibly, that the quality of instruction increases with the amount of money the university spent per student, and imagine two universities—one nonprofit, the other for-profit—neither of which starts with a financial endowment. Suppose the for-profit university charges $20,000 tuition and spends $20,000 on each student, giving it a profit of $0—just enough to keep going. The nonprofit university charges $18,000 in tuition and spends $20,000 on each student, requiring it to borrow $2,000 per student, money it expects to repay from future alumni donations.

Since the quality of instruction (as measured by expenditure per pupil) would be the same at both universities, a student should be indifferent between paying $20,000 to attend the for-profit university or paying a combination of current tuition and gifts worth the same amount to attend the nonprofit university. To illustrate, suppose the student's marginal income tax rate is 50 percent. Money he donates is tax deductible, so he could donate $4,000 to a nonprofit university and still be no worse off than if he had paid an additional $2,000 in tuition to the for-profit university.

Once donations started rolling in, the nonprofit could spend $22,000 for every $18,000 it collected in tuition. Its for-profit counterpart, however, could still spend only $20,000 for every $20,000 it collected in tuition.

In sum, nonprofit institutions have an advantage over their for-profit counterparts because part of their revenue comes from tax-deductible gifts. Such institutions are thus able to spend more per student, even if for-profit institutions operate at zero profit.

If we have Blockbuster Video, why don't we have Blockbuster Book? (Up Lim)

When people want to watch a DVD, they typically rent one from a commercial lender—either a retail outlet like Blockbuster Video or an online distributor like Netflix. Commercial book rental libraries have existed in various places and times, but they are relatively rare. For the most part, we either buy books from commercial bookstores or borrow them without charge from public libraries. Why don't we rent books?

Part of the answer lies in the economic justification for governments spending tax dollars in support of public libraries. The cost-benefit test says that the socially efficient level of reading or any other activity is the one for which its marginal cost is equal to the sum of its private and social marginal benefits. Economists have argued that in addition to the personal benefit people reap from reading, there are also benefits to others in the community. Thus, for example, everyone tends to benefit from the existence of a more well-informed citizenry. But individual consumers focus primarily on their own personal benefits when deciding whether to read a book, while ignoring any benefits that might accrue to others. People may thus tend to read fewer books than might be justified if the cost-benefit test were applied from the perspective of the community as a whole. A natural remedy is to make reading books more attractive by subsiding them—and hence the attraction of public libraries.

Of course, a similar argument might be advanced on behalf of specific films. Some have claimed, for example, that films like *An Inconvenient Truth* produce a better-informed electorate, which should eventually lead to more intelligent public policies on global climate change. On balance, however, the consensus is that films serve this broader educational mission to a significantly lesser extent than books do, and are therefore less deserving of public support.

Another reason that commercial book rentals are far less common than commercial movie rentals is that whereas movies can usually be watched in under two hours, it often takes several days, sometimes several weeks, to read a book. As a result of longer turnover times for books, the rental fee necessary for a book rental store to break even might thus have to be several times higher than for a movie rental store. Yet as in the case of wedding gowns, rental fees can rise only so high before buying becomes more attractive than renting.

As we saw in the preceding chapter, behaviors that serve the narrow interests of individuals often harm the interests of the groups to which they belong. When that happens among nonhuman animals, there is generally no remedy. Although male elk would have intelligible reasons for entering an agreement calling for each animal to have his antlers trimmed back by half, there is no practical way for them to implement such an agreement.

In human groups, of course, things are different. When individual incentives favor behaviors that harm groups, we can mitigate the conflict. As we saw in the previous chapter, hockey players routinely empower their leagues to enforce rules requiring helmets, even though they invariably skate without them in the absence of such rules. The following examples illustrate similar ways in which laws and regulations can help resolve conflicts between individual and group interests.

Why do workers vote for politicians who favor workplace safety regulations, even though, when left to their own devices, they almost invariably choose less safe jobs paying higher wages?

The conventional explanation is that regulations are needed to prevent workers from being exploited by employers with market power. Yet safety regulations bind most tightly in the same labor markets that are most highly competitive. The cost-benefit test for a safety device is whether workers would be willing to pay its cost. If a device that met this test were not provided in a competitive market, there would be cash on the table. Suppose, for example, that workers were willing to sacrifice $100 a week in wages for the extra safety provided by a device costing only $50 a week. If an employer failed to offer the device, there would be cash on the table available to a rival employer who offered it and paid for it by offering wages that were, say, $60 lower than those paid by the first employer. Both the workers who moved to the new firm and the new firm itself would come out ahead. In sum, if workers want more safety and are willing to bear its cost, firms should have an incentive to provide it even in the absence of regulation. So why regulate?

Thomas Schelling's hockey helmet example (Chapter 5) suggests that workers might find it attractive to limit their own choices in the realm of safety. As in hockey, many of the most important outcomes in life depend on relative position. Because a "good" school is an inescapably relative concept, each family's quest to provide a better education for its children has much in common with the athlete's quest for competitive advantage. Families try to buy houses in the best school districts they can afford; yet when all families spend more, the result is merely to bid up the prices of those houses. Half of all children must still attend bottom-half schools.

Riskier jobs pay higher wages because employers spend less on safety. Workers can thus gain a financial advantage by accepting such jobs, which enable them to bid more effectively for houses in better school districts. Just as unrestricted hockey players may feel compelled to discard their helmets, workers who are free to sell their safety for higher wages may realize that unless they do so, they will consign their children to inferior schools. In each case, limiting one's options can prevent a mutually disadvantageous race to the bottom.

Why does the Fair Labor Standards Act make it illegal for consenting adults to work overtime at whatever wage they choose? *(George Akerlof)*

The Fair Labor Standards Act requires employers to pay overtime premiums for all hours worked in excess of forty per week. Free market economists often denounce this requirement, noting that many people would voluntarily work the longer hours employers would have offered in the absence of premiums. Because of the disincentive implicit in the premium, most employers offer overtime work only to meet unforeseen production shortfalls, which occur infrequently. Why does the law prevent workers and employees from entering into contracts they find mutually beneficial?

The logic of requiring employers to pay overtime wage premiums may be similar to the logic of requiring employers to limit workplace safety risks. Thus individuals can often increase their odds of promotion by working longer hours, but when others follow suit, everyone's promotion prospects remain roughly the same as before. The result is often a rat race in which all must work until eight each evening merely to avoid falling behind.

Even when promotion is not at issue, the individual's incentives to work longer hours can be misleadingly attractive from the perspective of the larger group. For instance, when an individual works longer hours, that individual can afford to buy a house in a better school district; but when all work longer hours, the effect is merely to bid up the prices of houses in the better school districts. As before, half of all children must attend schools in the bottom half.

Adam Smith's invisible hand rests on the implicit premise that individual rewards depend only on absolute performance. The plain fact, however, is that much of life is graded on the curve.

Why were superthin models banned from Madrid's annual fashion week?

In September 2006, the organizers of Madrid's annual fashion week, known as Pasarela Cibeles, reached an agreement with the Association of Fashion Designers of Spain that banned the appearance of any runway model with a body mass index (BMI) of 18 or lower. (A model standing 5 feet 9 inches would need to weigh about 125 pounds to achieve a BMI of 18.) Organizers of Madrid's fashion week said they wanted their event to project "an image of beauty and health." Yet consumers obviously find thinner fashion models more beautiful than others, or else designers wouldn't hire them. So why ban skinny models?

Photo by Bernat Armangue / AP.

Ultrathin models: No longer permitted in Madrid's Pasarela Cibeles fashion show.

Designers believe, and the public seems to agree, that clothing drapes more gracefully on slender models. Up to a point, therefore, a designer can gain competitive advantage by employing thinner models. To remain competitive, other designers must follow suit, and the ensuing positional arms race may dictate eating habits that threaten models' health. A plausible rationale for the BMI rule is that it helps defuse this arms race.

British Culture Secretary Tessa Jowell applauded the Madrid rule and urged the organizers of London Fashion Week to adopt it, arguing that its impact would extend far beyond the fashion industry. "Young girls aspire to look like the catwalk models," she said. "When those models are unhealthily underweight it pressurizes girls to starve themselves to look the same."

Why do most states enforce mandatory kindergarten start dates?

Most jurisdictions have laws that require children to start kindergarten by the age of six. Yet children of that age vary enormously in terms of their physical, intellectual, and emotional maturity. Why don't states leave it up to parents to decide when their children are ready to start school?

Suppose most children started kindergarten at age six, and a couple had the option of holding their own six-year-old son out for an extra year. By starting as a seven-year-old, he would be bigger, stronger, smarter, and more mature relative to his classmates. And since performance in all domains of school is graded on the curve, the child could expect to receive better grades, be more likely to succeed on athletic teams, and be more likely to occupy positions of leadership in school organizations. In short, he would be launched on a path that would make admission to an elite college or university more likely.

But when one individual moves forward in relative terms, others move back. Other ambitious parents would feel pressure to keep their six-year-olds at home another year. No matter how ambitious parents were, they would not keep holding their children back indefinitely. But it is possible to imagine an average start date of eight or nine years of age in jurisdictions that left parents free to choose. And since there is no gain, from the collective vantage point, when all children start school later, most jurisdictions have decided not to leave that decision up to individual parents.

THE FACT THAT INDIVIDUAL INCENTIVES do not coincide with collective incentives is of course not the only reason that countries regulate behavior. In the domain of safety, for example, many have argued that individuals often lack the necessary information, or perhaps even the required foresight, to make intelligent choices.

Such paternalistic regulation is often controversial. But it is generally more likely to be embraced when it applies to children, since most adults agree that children are not well positioned to make intelligent safety decisions on their own. As the following examples illustrate, however, the cost-benefit principle still plays a central role in decisions about the specific forms these regulations should take.

Why are child safety seats required in cars but not in airplanes? *(Greg Balet)*

In your car, the government requires that your child be fastened securely into a safety seat of approved design, even for a short drive to the grocery store. Yet you can keep a child under two on your lap untethered when you fly from New York to Los Angeles. What explains this difference?

Some have attributed it to the fact that if the plane crashes, you are going to die anyway, strapped in or not. That is true, but there are many other things happen short of a crash—severe air turbulence, for example—for which being belted in helps a lot.

A more plausible explanation begins with the observation that, once you have a child safety seat, it is costless to strap your child into it in the backseat of your car because there is almost always enough room for it. Since the marginal cost is zero and the marginal benefit is improved safety for your child, strapping your child in while traveling in your car makes perfect sense. If you are on a full flight from New York to Los Angeles, however, you must buy an extra ticket in order to strap your child into a safety seat, which might cost you $1,000 (even with a Saturday stayover).

Drawing by Mick Stevens.

The opportunity cost of using a safety seat is much lower in cars than on a full flight.

People may not feel comfortable saying that it is too expensive to provide the extra safety for their children when traveling by air, but that is essentially what it boils down to. So they hold tight to their children and hope for the best, rather than pay $1,000 for an extra seat.

Why are seat belts required in cars but not in school buses? *(Carole Scarzella, Tanvee Mehra, Jim Siahaan, and Sachin Das)*

Every state except New Hampshire ("Live Free or Die!") has a law requiring automobile drivers and passengers to wear seat belts. But only four states (New York, New Jersey, Florida, and California) require that seat belts be installed on all new school buses. Why this difference?

According to the National Highway Traffic Safety Administration, the use of seat belts in cars saves more than 12,000 lives a year. With traffic fatalities still in excess of 40,000 a year, this is a huge savings. But although one in eight of these fatalities is under the age of nineteen—more than 5,000 deaths a year—the death rate for children in school buses is dramatically lower, averaging 10.2 deaths per year between 1990 and 2000. A 2002 study by the National Research Council reported that traveling to school on foot, on a bicycle, or in a car involves far more risk than riding in a school bus. Liz Neblett of the National Highway Traffic Safety Administration, noting that school buses have tightly compartmentalized seating with tall, shock-absorbing backrests, said that "a school bus holds children like eggs in an egg crate. It is the safest form of transportation on the road."

The cost of adding seat belts to a typical school bus has been estimated to be approximately $1,800. Available evidence suggests that many more lives would be saved if the same money were spent on improving the safety of pedestrian crossings near school bus stops.

Why do pleasure boats have more limited collision safety equipment than automobiles? *(Peter Gyozo)*

Under federal regulations, most cars sold today are equipped with driver's and passenger's side airbags, three-point seat belts, and energy-absorbing features that help dissipate the destructive forces generated by high-speed collisions. Why don't regulations require similar features on recreational power boats?

Almost all boat users also drive cars. From the perspective of both rational individuals and rational regulators, the criterion for optimal safety investment is for the last dollar spent on safety in each domain to yield the same increment in the probability of surviving. (Suppose the last dollar a boat owner spent on safety equipment for his car yielded a smaller increase in survival probability than the last dollar spent on safety equipment for his boat. He could then increase his survival probability by spending a dollar less on car safety and a dollar more on boat safety.)

For a variety of reasons, a given safety device tends to yield much higher gain if installed in a car than in a boat. Most important, the typical driver spends several hundred hours a year behind the wheel of his car, but few boat owners, especially in northern climates, log even forty hours a year in their boats. The cost of installing a safety device is the same, no matter how many hours the car or boat is used. So the number of lives saved per safety device tends to be much higher in cars than in boats. (Note the similarity between this explanation and the one in Chapter 2 for why it makes more sense to have a light in the refrigerator than in the freezer.)

Safety devices also tend to matter less in boats because the waterways are less congested, on average, than highways, and because boats travel at much lower average speeds than cars. Harbors, canals, and other high-traffic areas often have speed limits of 5 MPH—a speed at which collisions seldom result in injury.

The point is not that boating is a risk-free activity. More than eight hundred persons are killed each year in boating accidents in the United States. And indeed, boat owners are required to invest in specific safety equipment that has been shown to have significant impact on the survival chances of boaters. Most states, for example, require boats to carry one Coast Guard–approved personal flotation device for each person onboard. The bottom line, however, is that automobile travel is far riskier than boat travel, so it makes good economic sense to invest more heavily in auto safety devices.

ONE INFLUENTIAL SCHOOL of economic thought holds that law evolves in ways that promote efficiency. An efficient law is defined as one that maximizes the wealth of members of society. The appeal of this idea is that if there were two alternative ways to write a law and one was more efficient than the other, it should be possible to strike a deal that makes everyone better off under the efficient law than they would have been under the inefficient one.

Suppose, for example, that one version of a law would increase consumers' total wealth by $3 billion and have no effect on producers' wealth, while another version of the same law would increase the wealth of producers by $1 billion and have no effect on consumers. The first alternative is the efficient one because it produces the larger total increase in wealth.

But suppose producers had the political power to force adoption of the second alternative. Proponents of the legal efficiency hypothesis argue that producers would prefer to use that power to extract tax breaks sufficient to compensate for the $1 billion they would sacrifice by agreeing to the efficient version of the law.

A competing school of thought concedes the attractiveness of this argument but emphasizes that the negotiations needed to reach efficient outcomes are often difficult to carry out in practice. The upshot, according to this view, is that laws and regulations are sometimes enacted not because they promote efficiency but because they serve powerful special interests.

As many of the examples above suggest, the pro-efficiency view has much to commend it. But the special interests view is not without explanatory power of its own.

Why is it legal to drive while eating a cheeseburger or drinking coffee but not while talking on a cell phone? *(Evan Psaropoulos)*

Evidence that using a cell phone while driving increases the motorist's likelihood of having an accident has led many states to ban the practice, with exceptions in some states for cell phones with headsets that allow hands-free use. Yet drivers may legally engage in other activities that appear to be at least as hazardous: eating fast food, drinking hot beverages, changing CDs, even applying cosmetics. Since such activities present visual and mechanical distractions similar to those associated with cell phone use, why aren't they also illegal?

One possible reason is that cell phone use is more distracting than those other activities. Drivers who become engaged in conversation, for instance, may become much less attentive than those who are merely eating a hamburger. Yet talking with other passengers in the car remains legal. Some have claimed that talking on a cell phone is more distracting than talking with a passenger, who can tell when traffic conditions dictate interrupting the conversation. But since regulators in most states still permit cell phone use with headsets, that explanation also seems insufficient.

When all other attempts to explain the rationale for a law fail, a good strategy is to ask how it might change the income of those affected by it. If legislators banned the consumption of coffee and hamburgers while driving, sales at fast food restaurants would plummet. Legislators might thus be reluctant to enact such a law for fear that corporations would retaliate by withholding campaign contributions. By allowing the headset exception to the ban on cell phone use while driving, legislators do not run that risk, since wireless providers can sell just as many subscriptions as before. Indeed, they may even earn higher profits through the sale of additional headsets.

Another contributing factor may be that eating while driving is a practice that became established long before society began to impose detailed safety regulations on personal conduct. Talking on cell phones and other emerging risky behaviors may thus be more tempting targets for regulators. Here again, history matters.

Why isn't the use of radar detectors illegal in all fifty states? *(Matt Rosedale)*

Highway speed limits are imposed in every U.S. jurisdiction because people believe that allowing drivers to drive as fast as they please would pose unacceptable risks to public safety. Federal law prohibits the use of radar detectors in commercial vehicles involved in interstate commerce, but only Virginia and the District of Columbia outlaw their use in passenger vehicles. Given at least grudging public support for having speed limits, why do so many state legislatures refuse to outlaw a device whose only purpose is to enable motorists to evade them?

In fact state legislatures have tried many times to introduce laws banning radar detectors. According to the Radio Association Defending Airwave Rights (RADAR), a pro-detector lobbying group, more than 110 attempts to ban radar detectors in 33 states have been defeated in recent years. So one possible explanation for the legality of radar detectors is that a few powerful economic actors (sellers of radar detectors) have a strong incentive to lobby against prohibitions.

In contrast, the public interest in enacting prohibitions against radar detectors is diffuse. Few consumers take enough interest in this issue to bother writing their elected representatives about it, and fewer still are prepared to make or withhold significant campaign contributions on the basis of it.

In addition, many motorists appear ambivalent about whether radar detectors should be illegal. Surveys consistently show, for example, that more than 90 percent of all people believe themselves to be above-average drivers. (Psychologists call this the Lake Wobegon effect, after Garrison Keillor's mythical Midwest town where "all the children are above average.") So most drivers probably think that although speed limits are needed to protect against the incompetence of other drivers, they themselves can safely speed. In any event, most drivers appear more than willing to exploit opportunities to exceed posted speed limits. On interstate highways where the posted limit is sixty-five miles per hour, for example, many motorists set their cruise controls to seventy-four, having heard from someone who knows a state trooper that authorities ticket only those who exceed the limit by more than ten miles per hour. It is thus not surprising that states have found it so difficult to ban radar detectors.

THE FINAL TWO EXAMPLES in this chapter speak to how economic principles affect the design of laws intended to help protect consumers from abuse by firms with market power. Both focus on the taxi industry in New York, where the city government has created a legal monopoly by making it unlawful to operate a taxi without first purchasing a medallion, or operating license. In part to help relieve street congestion, the city issues only a limited number of medallions, which makes fewer taxis available than there would be if entry into the taxi market were unregulated.

One result is that medallion owners enjoy a measure of market power that, unchecked, would enable them to charge rates far in excess of the actual cost of ferrying passengers. And so it is common for cities to regulate not just the number of taxis that can operate but also the fares they are permitted to charge. The aim of these regulations is not just to protect consumers from unfair treatment but to promote more efficient decisions about taxi use.

Why do taxicab fees have both a fixed component and a variable component, instead of charging a higher rate for each mile traveled? *(Mario Caporicci)*

Under New York taxi regulations in 2006, cabs were permitted to charge their passengers a $2.50 fixed fee plus forty cents for each fifth of a mile traveled, plus forty cents for every two minutes waiting in traffic. Similar regulated fee structures are common in cities around the world. Why don't regulatory commissions instead adopt the seemingly simpler alternative of dispensing with the flat fee and charging higher rates for miles and waiting time?

Because taxis would use an electronic mileage meter to calculate their fares in either case, it would not really be simpler to base fares only on mileage traveled. A more compelling justification for the current fare structure is that it is more efficient than charging only for mileage.

To stay in business, taxi owners must cover all their costs. Some are roughly proportional to the number of miles traveled (fuel, maintenance, and depreciation, for example), but many others are not. The opportunity cost of money invested in their cabs, for example, is the same no matter how many miles they travel. It is the same for insurance expenses. And in cities that require taxis to be equipped with medallions, the market price of a medallion is also a fixed cost. (A medallion for a New York taxi currently sells for more than $300,000.)

The most efficient taxi rate structure is one that leads consumers to base their taxi use decisions as closely as possible on the *extra* costs their use causes drivers to incur. If a taxi had to cover all its costs from a rate that charged only according to the number of miles traveled, the rate might have to be several dollars per mile. This would discourage many people from taking cab rides covering more than just a short distance, even though the actual additional cost of serving those customers might be lower than what they were willing to pay.

A rate structure with both fixed and variable components more closely mimics the actual cost structure that most cabs confront. By enabling taxis to keep their charge per mile lower than would otherwise be possible, this rate structure does not force passengers to pay much more than the actual cost of long rides. It is thus less likely to dissuade people from taking long rides whose benefit exceeds their true cost.

Why is the taxi fare from John F. Kennedy Airport (JFK) to any destination in Manhattan a flat rate of $45, while most other cab rides in the city are metered fares? *(Travis Murphy Parsons)*

Depending on the density of traffic, metered fares from JFK airport to various destinations in Manhattan vary between $30 and $70 under the standard formula employed for taxi rides in almost all parts of the city. Why, then, have New York taxi regulators mandated a fixed fare of $45 from JFK to Manhattan?

JFK airport is one of the premier international gateways to the United States. Tourism is a major industry in New York, and the city has a strong interest in helping ensure that newly arrived foreign visitors have a positive experience. Because many of these visitors have a minimal command of English, they are especially vulnerable in commercial transactions, including those with taxi drivers. To prevent tourists and other inexperienced travelers from having to worry about whether taxi drivers are taking circuitous routes or finding other ways of charging them unfair prices, the New York City Taxi and Limousine Commission has set a flat rate for taxi service from JFK into Manhattan.

7

Decoding Marketplace Signals

Economists often assume that people and firms have complete information about the costs and benefits relevant to their decisions. In practice, however, we are often woefully ill informed, even when confronting important decisions. But the cost-benefit principle applies even in these cases, suggesting that acting on limited information is often better than bearing the expense of becoming more fully informed.

As the first example in this chapter illustrates, the decision maker's efforts to become informed are often complicated by the fact that those who possess the relevant information have no incentive to reveal it truthfully.

Why do stock analysts seldom recommend selling a particular company's stock? *(Joseph Lucarelli)*

Although the stock market as a whole gains value most years, the goal of ambitious investors is to do better than leading benchmarks, such as the Standard & Poors 500 Index. To that end, many rely on the recommendations of professional stock analysts. Yet studies show these recommendations to be astonishingly one-sided. In 2000, for example, there were 28,000 recommendations on U.S. companies by brokerage house analysts, of which more than 99 percent were either strong buy, buy, or hold. Analysts recommended selling the stocks of individual companies less than 1 percent of the time that year. Yet a substantial share of American companies saw their stock prices decline in 2000, many of them by more than half. Why are analysts' recommendations so heavily tilted toward buy?

It is tempting to say that analysts in 2000 fell victim to the same "irrational exuberance" that affected investors generally during the boom years of the late 1990s. But research shows that analyst recommendations show a similar bias toward optimism in other years as well.

A plausible source of this bias is suggested by an examination of the costs and benefits confronting stock analysts as they formulate their recommendations. Consider a stock that is covered by five different analysts. Each wants to make an accurate prediction of how the stock's price will move during the coming months, but each also wants to maintain a good relationship with the company being evaluated, often a client or a potential client of her employer.

All things considered, the analyst faces strong incentives to consider the likely recommendations of the other four analysts before formulating her own position. After all, she knows that the cost of being wrong depends in part on the recommendations made by the other four analysts. From the outset, she knows that the recommendations of others are likely to be biased at least slightly in favor of buying, because analysts' employers have an interest in currying favor with evaluated companies. At one extreme, if all five recommend buy and the company's stock price then falls, the analyst knows that her vulnerability to criticism will be limited by the fact that the forecast error was widespread.

Alternatively, if she recommends sell while the other four recommend buy and the company's stock price then goes up, she becomes a triple loser. Not only was her recommendation wrong, but her error was conspicuous, since rival analysts got it right. Adding insult to injury, her employer would suffer the ill will of a potential client.

Under the circumstances, the safest bet for the individual analyst is to herd with the expected recommendations of other analysts. Each understands that the interests of other analysts' employers are, like those of her own, better served through buy recommendations. In addition, other analysts are making forecasts not only of how the company's stock will perform but also of what other analysts will recommend. So it is easy to see why the analyst's safest bet is a buy recommendation. But as careful investors eventually learn, a buy recommendation conveys little useful information about a stock's future price.

IT IS MORE THE RULE than the exception for market transactions to occur between parties whose interests are at least potentially in conflict. The seller wants the buyer to reveal how much he is willing to pay, but the buyer, fearing that the seller will overcharge him, tries to conceal his enthusiasm. Similarly, the buyer wants to know whether the product he is considering is any good, but the seller, who knows, cannot be trusted to reveal its flaws. How can decision makers become better informed in such situations?

Biologists have employed basic economic principles in an attempt to answer this question in the case of animals whose interests are in conflict. When two dogs want the same bone, for example, each has a keen interest in discerning how formidable his rival is before deciding whether to fight. The fact that their adversaries cannot make declarative statements about how formidable they are is beside the point, since statements like "I'm formidable! You'd better not fight me for this bone!" would not be credible.

In this situation, dogs implicitly rely on the "costly to fake principle," which says that for a signal between potential adversaries to be credible, it must be costly (or at least difficult) to fake. Size is one such signal, since the larger a dog is, the more formidable he is likely to be as an adversary. When a dog confronts a significantly larger rival, he is likely to defer. But when his rival is significantly smaller, he is more willing to fight.

In these situations, dogs do their best to appear as large as they can. When they are emotionally aroused to do battle, the tiny nonstriated muscles that surround the hair follicles on their backs instantly contract, causing their hackles to stand upright, making them appear larger. But natural selection has seen to it that all surviving dogs follow this strategy, so in the end no one is really fooled by it. Dogs that look bigger, hackles and all, really are bigger.

The costly to fake principle also explains why the baby bird that screams the loudest in the nest is the one most likely to be fed by a parent returning with a worm. Each chick's interest is to get as much food as possible, and to that end it chirps loudly to signal its hunger. But because its siblings employ the same strategy, this signal might seem uninformative. Experiments have shown, however, that hungrier chicks are able to scream louder than others. Motivation counts for a lot here, and being really hungry provides the motivation necessary to produce the highest-decibel chirps.

THE COSTLY TO FAKE PRINCIPLE also applies to communications between potential adversaries in various market settings.

Why do producers sometimes put the phrase "As Seen on TV" in print ads and on some product packages? (Joan Moriarty)

Manufacturers who advertise their products on TV sometimes seem eager to make potential buyers aware of that fact. Thus they often include the phrase "As Seen on TV" in advertisements in newspapers and magazines and on product packaging. Why should buyers care whether a product has been seen on TV?

Television advertising can be enormously expensive, with thirty-second commercials selling for more than $2.5 million during some time slots. Not all TV ads are that expensive, of course. But even late-night ads on cable channels are generally much more expensive than ads in most radio and print outlets. So the real question is, Why are producers eager for people to know that they have invested heavily to call their products to the attention of potential buyers?

The key to answering this question is the observation that money spent on advertising yields a higher return for good products than for bad ones. The most an ad can do is induce potential buyers to try the product. If they try it and like it, then the ad has really paid off, for they are likely to become repeat purchasers and tell their friends about it. But if buyers try a product and find it disappointing, they won't buy it again and are unlikely to recommend it to friends. In the latter case, money spent on advertising is largely wasted.

Drawing by Mick Stevens.

Should anyone care?

Because producers generally do a significant amount of focus group testing before bringing products to market, they have a reasonably good idea which ones consumers will like best. So when a producer decides to invest heavily in advertising a product, potential buyers reasonably infer that the producer has good reason to expect consumers to like it. Otherwise it would not pay to spend heavily to advertise it. It is thus no mystery why many producers might want to call our attention to the fact that they have advertised their products on TV, the most expensive of all media.

Why do lawyers spend more on cars and clothing than college professors with the same income?

The more money people earn, the more they are likely to spend on most categories of consumption. Automobiles and clothing are no exceptions.

Dress is a more important signal of ability in some occupations than in others.

The rich spend much more on each than the poor. But income is not the sole determinant of such expenditures. Thus, for example, lawyers typically spend more on both cars and clothing than college professors with similar taste and income. Why this difference?

As noted, there is a positive link between how much money people earn and how much they spend. There is also a positive link between people's level of talent and the salary they command in competitive labor markets. Together, these relationships imply a positive link between how talented people are and how much they spend on cars and clothing. So one can make a crude guess about how talented a person is by looking at the kind of clothing he wears or the kind of car he drives.

This guess will be more accurate for people in some occupations than in others. Talented lawyers, for example, are much in demand and command high fees, whereas the most talented college professors often earn little more than their less talented colleagues. Differences in the amount spent on cars and clothing are thus more reliable signals of the underlying differences in talent among lawyers than college professors. A client shopping for a skilled lawyer would have ample reason to be wary of hiring one who drove a rusting ten-year-old Geo Metro. In contrast, a student would have no reason to be skeptical about the ability of a chemistry professor who drove the same car.

If the kind of car a lawyer drives is even a weak signal to potential clients about competence, lawyers will inevitably attempt to manipulate this signal by spending more on cars than they otherwise would have. Once the resulting expenditure arms race plays out, the most talented lawyers will still be driving the most expensive cars, on average. But many will end up spending more than they may have wished. Lawyers, in short, face greater pressure to spend on cars and clothing because it is more costly for them to send misleading signals about how good they are. A lawyer who failed to match his colleagues' spending would appear less able than he really was, just as a dog that failed to raise its hackles in battle would appear misleadingly small.

In contrast, none of the professional outcomes that professors care most about would become more likely if they spent more on clothing or cars. Professors want their papers published in leading journals and want their grant applications to be funded. But the people who make those decisions typically have no idea how a professor dresses or what he drives.

Why is there so much mathematical formalism in economics?

The use of formal mathematical models has a long and distinguished history in economics and has generated powerful insights into how markets function. But since the middle of the twentieth century, the level of mathematical formalism in economics has escalated sharply, leading even many within the profession to conclude that it has become excessive. Have economists gone overboard in their use of math?

The escalation of mathematical formalism coincided with increasingly stiff competition for academic jobs. In a profession that prizes rigor, being perceived as the more rigorous of two candidates is advantageous. Formulating and manipulating sophisticated mathematical models are not tasks for the intellectually faint of heart. By accomplishing

Given this choice of $f(p, q; \alpha)$, the density for persons employed on the date of the survey may be written, using equation (8) from the previous section, as

$$(30) \qquad g(p, q) = \frac{p+q}{E(R)} f(p, q) = \frac{k}{E(R)} q^{\alpha_1 - 1} (1-q)^{\alpha_2 - 1} p^{\alpha_3} (1-p)^{\alpha_4 - 1},$$

where the fact that $\int_p \int_q g(p, q) = 1$ may be used to determine that

$$(31) \qquad E(R) = \frac{\dfrac{\alpha_3}{\alpha_3 + \alpha_4}}{\dfrac{\alpha_1}{\alpha_1 + \alpha_2} + \dfrac{\alpha_3}{\alpha_3 + \alpha_4}} = \bar{R}(\alpha).$$

Using equation (9), the density for persons unemployed on the date of the survey may be written as

$$(32) \qquad h(p, q) = \frac{q}{\dfrac{p+q}{1 - E(R)}} = \frac{k}{1 - E(R)} q^{\alpha_1} (1-q)^{\alpha_2 - 1} p^{\alpha_3 - 1} (1-p)^{\alpha_4 - 1}.^{11}$$

The density for the starting cohort is given by

$$(33) \qquad m(p, q) = k^* q^{\alpha_1} (1-q)^{\alpha_2 - 1} p^{\alpha_3} (1-p)^{\alpha_4 - 1},$$

Mathematical formalism in economics: Too much of a good thing?

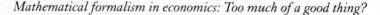

them, a candidate credibly signals his or her prowess. So candidates have an obvious incentive to invest additional time and effort in honing their mathematical skills.

But here as elsewhere, the strength of a signal depends on context. As more and more economists increase the level of formalism in their work, the threshold for signaling intellectual prowess gradually rises. The resulting arms race may lead to excessive formalism.

The level of mathematical formalism in economics may thus be too high for the same reason that people tend to raise their voices at cocktail parties. In a crowded space with high ambient noise levels, one must speak up simply to be heard. But when all speak in louder voices, the ambient noise level rises, making it necessary to speak still more loudly.

Why do humanities professors, who should be more adept than most in their use of language, often write so unclearly?

Members of most groups exhibit enormous variability in their ability to communicate. This is true even among politicians, whose success depends heavily on that ability. Some, like Bill Clinton, are models of clarity, while others, like George W. Bush, are often difficult to understand. Members of other groups, however, show little variation in verbal ability. It is extremely difficult, for example, to become a humanities professor without demonstrating prodigious facility in both written and spoken language. Yet barely intelligible passages abound in the professional writings of humanities professors. For instance, in an article entitled "Tactical Strategies of the Streetwalker," Maria Lugones writes,

> I propose to embrace tactical strategies in moving in disruption of the dichotomy, as crucial to an epistemology of resistance/liberation. To do so is to give uptake to the disaggregation of collectivity concomitant with social fragmentation and to theorize the navigation of its perils without giving uptake to its logic.

Perhaps most humanities professors are able to decode this passage without difficulty, but an informal survey reveals that most others cannot. Why are the writings of humanities professors so often opaque to ordinary readers?

One hypothesis is that modes of discourse in the humanities are molded by forces similar to those that mold discourse in economics. Just as it is in an economist's interest to appear rigorous in comparison with competing job candidates, it is in a humanities professor's interest to appear erudite. In an initial condition in which most humanities professors spoke and wrote in clear English sentences, it is easy to imagine that an individual professor might gain advantage by inserting the occasional unfamiliar word or expression into her writings. Doing so, after all, would convey the impression that she spoke with authority, since she evidently knew something the reader didn't.

It wouldn't do, of course, to insert too many unfamiliar words or expressions, for then readers would complain that the writing was unintelligible. But as others gradually began inserting their own displays of erudition, many once unfamiliar words and expressions would eventually be more broadly understood by professional audiences. At that point, an individual writer would have to push the envelope still further in order to convey erudition. And as more and more did so, the standards that define intelligibility among professional readers would begin to shift. When the dust settles—if it ever does—it would be no surprise that the professional writings of humanities professors might bear little resemblance to conventional written English.

It is sometimes said that there are two kinds of buyers in the marketplace, those who don't know what they're doing and those who don't know that they don't know what they're doing. Buyers of the first type can sometimes limit their losses by taking account of what their lack of knowledge implies about observable links between price and quality. Both of the following examples involve asymmetric information. The seller knows much more about the quality of the product than the prospective buyer does. The buyer's task in each case is to infer from the seller's observable behavior how good the product is likely to be.

Why do "almost new" used cars sell for so much less than brand-new ones? (George Akerlof)

When a new car leaves the showroom, it can lose 20 percent or more of its value almost overnight. Considering that modern cars typically have useful lives of more than 200,000 miles, why should a few miles on the odometer cause a vehicle's price to plummet?

Part of the price drop reflects the difference between wholesale and retail prices. When a new car is first sold, the buyer pays retail price, which can be as much as 15 percent higher than what the dealer paid for it. When a private consumer buys a car and decides to sell it immediately, he becomes an amateur car dealer. He would like to sell the car at close to its original retail price, of course. But in attempting to do so, he must compete with a host of professional dealers who have attractive, well-lighted showrooms and employ skilled salespersons and mechanics. And because it is easier for professional dealers to attract interested car buyers, it is to be expected that the offerings of private sellers will command lower prices.

But there is a second important reason that nearly new used cars sell for so much less than brand-new ones. Because of variations in manufacturing and assembly processes, not all new cars are equally reliable when they come off the assembly line. Such differences in reliability are amplified by differences in the care with which owners maintain their vehicles. Although some almost new cars are lemons, not even trained mechanics can distinguish them from their more reliable counterparts. The upshot is that the owner of a used car generally knows much more about it than a prospective buyer does.

This asymmetry can have dramatic implications for the pricing of used cars. To illustrate, suppose the typical person values a reliable used car at $20,000 and an unreliable one at $10,000; suppose further that half of all used cars are reliable, making the average value of all used cars $15,000.

Under these circumstances, used cars would sell for much less than $15,000. To see why, suppose they all sold for $15,000. What kinds of used cars would then be offered? If people value reliable used cars at $20,000, as assumed, no owner of a reliable car would offer it for sale at a lower price. In contrast, owners of unreliable cars would be only too happy to sell them for $15,000, since they value such cars at only $10,000. The only used cars offered for sale would thus be unreliable ones. So people would be unwilling to buy used cars unless their price was deeply discounted.

In reality, of course, some used cars are sold for reasons that have nothing to do with their reliability. In such cases, sellers take pains to communicate that factors beyond their control led them to put their cars up for sale. ("Got transferred to London, must sell my Volvo station wagon.". . . "Just had a baby, must sell my Porsche Boxster.")

Why are Australian films so successful?

What do the following items have in common? *Breaker Morant, Picnic at Hanging Rock, The Last Wave, Strictly Ballroom, Priscilla, Queen of the Desert, My Brilliant Career, Mad Max, Gallipoli, Moulin Rouge, Walkabout, Lantana, Rabbit Proof Fence, The Year of Living Dangerously, Muriel's Wedding, Shine,* and *Crocodile Dundee.*

Each is a film made in Australia, and each attracted large, appreciative audiences in the United States. Most of these films were produced on modest budgets. As a group, they were far more successful than the average American film, which is produced on a much larger budget. What accounts for the success of Australian films shown in the United States?

Some conjecture that Australian culture is more nurturing of creative endeavor than American culture. But a simpler explanation is worth considering—the Australian films shown in the United States are not a representative sample of all recent Australian films.

It is more expensive to launch a film in the American market than in any other market. Advertising budgets alone often exceed tens of millions of dollars. Film industry executives are willing to invest that much only if there is a reasonable expectation that a film will attract a large audience. Many factors influence the decision of whether to see a particular film. A popular actor or a well-known director can lead many to buy a ticket. Sequels to popular films start with a ready-made audience. And favorable reviews clearly help. But perhaps most important of all, people attend films because of word of mouth.

When the Australian films on the list above first appeared in the United States, most American moviegoers had never heard of the directors or actors involved in them (although many, like Peter Weir and Mel Gibson, have gone on to become household names). Nor were these films sequels.

To succeed in the United States, their only hope was to be good enough to ensure critical acclaim and positive word of mouth. So the average quality of Australian films may seem so high to Americans simply because only the best films from down under made it to American shores.

COMPOUNDING THE PROBLEMS facing uninformed economic decision makers is the fact that readily available information does not always convey what it seems to. Sometimes available information is not very informative. If it predicts that quality is higher than it appears on some occasions and lower than it appears on others, little can be done. Sometimes, however, available information paints a systematically misleading picture. And as the following examples illustrate, economic decision makers can often profit in such cases by being aware of the direction of the resulting bias.

Why does the rookie of the year in baseball often have a less successful second season?

In 2002 rookie third baseman Eric Hinske batted .279 for the Toronto Blue Jays, with twenty-four home runs and eighty-four RBIs in 151 games, a performance that earned him the American League's Rookie of the Year Award. But in the following two seasons he batted only .243 and .248. This pattern is by no means unusual. Players named rookie of the year in Major League Baseball typically post records in their first season that would be creditable for established veteran players. But despite the advantage of having an additional year of experience, they often fail to match their rookie performance during their second year in the big leagues. Their decline in productivity occurs so regularly that it has a name: "sophomore slump." What accounts for it?

One possibility is that it takes time for opposing pitchers to discover a hitter's weaknesses. But if that were the explanation, it would apply to all second-year players, not just former rookies of the year. Yet second-year players as a group generally do slightly better than first-year players.

A more plausible explanation is that the sophomore slump is merely a statistical illusion. Even the best players do not perform with perfect consistency. Their batting averages and other offensive statistics are much higher in some seasons than in others. By definition, only players who have an exceptional season win the rookie of the year award. Thus their second year in the big leagues comes right after a year in which they may well have performed much better than their eventual career averages. It is therefore no surprise that their second season numbers are somewhat lower.

The sophomore slump is an example of what statisticians call regression to the mean. It occurs reliably whenever there is a random component to success. An unusually successful outing isn't always followed by a more nearly normal one. But more often than not it is.

Why does the strategy of firing the leader of a organization that performs poorly seem misleadingly attractive to organization officials?

When a professional athletic team has a losing season, often the team owner's immediate impulse is to fire the coach or manager. Similarly, when a corporation suffers deep losses, the first impulse of the board of directors is to fire the CEO. Does the fact that teams and corporations generally perform better under their new leaders during the following year attest to the wisdom of this strategy?

Losing seasons in sports, like unprofitable years in business, are typically the result of many factors. The leader's performance may be responsible in part, but in a really bad year it is likely that a number of other unfavorable factors were also in play. Those factors typically exhibit random fluctuations of their own, independent of who the manager or CEO might be. If they were extremely unfavorable in any one year, they are likely to be closer to the center of their normal range the next.

That new leaders are typically hired after bad years thus implies that we should expect to see better performance the following year, even if the new leader is no better than the old one. This improvement is just another example of regression to the mean. Of course, the previous leader might have performed miserably and deserved to be fired. But the mere fact that organizational performance usually rebounds in the wake of such firings is not evidence that firing the manager was the right move.

Why do managers tend to overestimate the efficacy of blame and underestimate the efficacy of praise?

Tough managers are quick to criticize their employees when they make mistakes and slow to praise them when they do well. In contrast, nurturing managers are quick to praise and slow to criticize. Which style is more effective? Because there is no one correct answer, managers new to their jobs have a natural tendency to experiment as they develop a style that works best for them. But such experiments have a built-in bias. They will lead many managers to conclude that praise is less effective, and blame more effective, than is actually the case. What accounts for this bias?

The explanation involves the same statistical phenomenon—regression to the mean—that accounts for the sophomore slump of rookies of the year. Employees, like baseball players, do not perform to the same standard at every moment. Some weeks they perform above their long-run average, other weeks below. Irrespective of the managerial feedback she receives, an employee who performs below her standard in one week is likely to improve—have a more nearly normal performance— the next. Conversely, an employee who performs above her standard one week is likely to fall back a bit the next, whether her manager praises her or not.

The upshot is that managers who are highly critical of employees following a subpar performance may misattribute the improved subsequent performance (which would have occurred anyway) to their tough feedback. Conversely, managers who praise their employees following superior performances may misinterpret the subsequent declines (which also would have occurred anyway) to their lenient management style.

Experiments suggest that in at least some settings, a nurturing managerial style is more likely to elicit good performance from employees than a highly critical style. Such evidence may be more reliable than casual impressions biased by regression to the mean.

As THIS CHAPTER's final example illustrates, the cost-benefit principle can sometimes help us make sense of information that seems transparently meaningless.

Why do stores post signs in their windows saying that guide dogs are permitted inside? *(Maurice Hernandez)*

Many stores post signs in their windows to advise customers of store policies. Some, for example, do not allow customers to enter without shoes or shirts, and it is increasingly common for stores to prohibit smoking and pets. When pets are prohibited, however, stores almost always post an additional notice saying that guide dogs are permitted.

Since neither guide dogs nor their owners can read these signs, why post them?

Sighted customers do not own guide dogs and thus have no direct need to know that the dogs are permitted. Even so, it may be advantageous for business owners that such customers know about the exemption for guide dogs. Some might see a dog in the store and, not recognizing it as a guide dog, erroneously conclude that the store was lax in enforcing its no-pets policy. Others might think a blanket exclusion of all pets unreasonable, on the grounds that it would discriminate against blind shoppers.

The magnitude of these benefits is admittedly slight. But the signs themselves, which are typically decals, cost next to nothing. So it may make sense to post them if they create even minimal benefits.

8

The Economic
Naturalist Hits the Road

T he details of economic life play out differently in different countries. For example, houses are substantially smaller in Japan than in the United States. While such differences are often attributed to culture, this begs the question of why cultures differ. Are the differences simply consequences of arbitrary variations in customs that emerged thousands of years ago? Psychologist Jerome Kagan has argued that many cultural norms are more fruitfully viewed as adaptations to the mix of problems that people confront at different times and in different places. In societies with a high child mortality rate, he notes, cultures tend to celebrate stoicism and detachment; those with frequent wars celebrate courage, and so on.

In Kagan's spirit, this chapter looks at differences in international behavior as consequences of disparities in the relevant costs and benefits. One of the most obvious differences among countries is in per capita incomes. People with different incomes often make different choices, whatever their cultural backgrounds.

Why is text messaging more common in most Asian countries than in the United States? *(Vivek Sethia, Kalyan Jonnalagadda)*

Travel in any Asian country and you'll see people of all ages busily typing text messages to one another on their cell phones. In the United States and Europe, however, text messaging is far less common. What explains this difference?

Because many countries in Asia had less well developed conventional telephone networks than the United States until recently, cell phone usage became widespread there sooner than in the United States. Text messaging uses far less bandwidth than voice messaging, so it can be offered at lower rates. With the exception of Japan, other Asian countries have significantly lower per capita incomes than the United States, so Asians were more likely to purchase text messaging plans.

As anyone who has ever tried it can testify, sending text messages on a cell phone keyboard is a skill that takes time and effort to develop. Having had long experience with this mode of communication, early Asian adopters have continued to exploit this skill, even though many now can afford voice communication. Wealthier Americans, having started with voice messaging from the outset, have little incentive to expend the effort necessary to become proficient in text messaging.

To this explanation, some might object that text messaging is common in at least some other countries, like Finland, which have long had well-developed conventional phone networks. But perhaps the Finns' affinity for text messaging stems from their famously nongregarious national character. "How do you identify a Finnish extrovert?" a wag asks. "Easy, he's the one who looks at *your* shoes."

Why is the proportion of aluminum cans recycled in Brazil much higher than in the United States? *(Luiz Fernando, Varga Buzolin)*

In the United States, consumers in eleven states must pay a deposit of five cents or more for every aluminum beverage can they buy, and frequent public service announcements urge them to recycle their beverage containers. To reclaim their deposits, consumers need only return the cans to a convenient recycling center. Most large grocery stores accept recycled cans, as do many other places. Yet only slightly more than half of the 70 billion aluminum beverage cans sold in the United States each year are recycled. Most of the rest end up in landfills. In contrast, there are no deposits charged on aluminum beverage cans sold in Brazil; nor are there convenient recycling centers. Nor does the Brazilian government broadcast public service announcements urging consumers to recycle used cans. Yet almost 90 percent of the aluminum beverage cans sold in Brazil are recycled each year. Why do Brazilians recycle at much higher rates than Americans?

Even though Brazil does not have a deposit system or conveniently located recycling centers, aluminum beverage containers can be sold for cash to entrepreneurs who melt them down and sell the recovered aluminum. Because average income in Brazil is less than 20 percent of the average income in the United States and extreme poverty is widespread, almost 200,000 people in Brazil make their principal living scavenging aluminum cans. By contrast, many Americans find it not worth their time to stand on line at recycling redemption centers, so their used cans often end up buried in landfills. According to Pat Franklin of the Container Recycling Institute, such discards have accounted for 11 million tons of aluminum cans over the past two decades, with an estimated value of $12 billion.

Although deposit laws have not produced universal recycling in the United States, they have had one desirable effect: aluminum cans that are discarded in public places are almost immediately picked up by scavengers. Unlike Brazilian scavengers, however, few American scavengers search for cans in landfills, which is illegal in many U.S. jurisdictions.

ALTHOUGH AVERAGE INCOMES in Asia are lower than in the United States and Europe, land prices in many Asian countries tend to be much higher, a consequence of higher population density in Asia. These price differences have interesting consequences for the entertainment industry.

Why do movie theaters in Korea and many other Asian countries have reserved seating, whereas American movie theaters generally have open seating? (Gloria Kim)

Moviegoers in Seoul, South Korea, buy tickets that assign specific seats in the theater. Their counterparts in Chicago, Illinois, can claim any open seat on a first-come, first-served basis. Why this difference?

Irrespective of location, reserved seating entails costs. Ticket sellers must query patrons about their seating preferences, for example, and ushers must direct patrons to the correct seats and resolve disputes when more than one person claims a given seat. These costs are roughly the same worldwide. This particular international difference is thus more likely to be rooted in international differences in the benefits of reserved seating.

In any city with a given population, there are many more screenings of each film in American movie theaters than in Asian ones. Having more screenings benefits moviegoers in at least two ways. One is that they are more likely to find a film at a time that suits them. A second is that theaters will usually have a significant number of empty seats at each screening, which makes it easier for moviegoers to decide to see a film at the last minute.

Screenings are typically less frequent in Asian theaters both because average incomes are lower and because land prices are higher, relative to average incomes, in Asian than in American cities. More frequent screenings raise costs, and people with lower incomes are naturally less willing to pay for the additional convenience they provide. Higher land prices in Asia make it more expensive to build theaters there, which further limits the frequency of screenings.

The upshot is that with so many fewer screenings, films shown in Asian theaters sell out much of the time. And when moviegoers expect a film to be sold out, their natural response is to show up early to be sure of getting a seat. The inevitable result is long waiting lines before screening time. Because these lines do nothing to increase the supply of available seats, the time people spend in them is wasted from the collective vantage point. Yet any individual who declined to wait in line would never get to see a film. (This is another example of conflict between individual and group interests.)

Reserved seating is a simple solution to this problem. When patrons can buy reserved-seat tickets well in advance, everyone is assured of getting a seat without having to stand in line for hours.

Why do American multiplexes generally allow customers to watch more than one movie for a single ticket, whereas Asian multiplexes allow only one movie per ticket? *(Frank Fu)*

Although they do not advertise the fact, most American movie theaters do not prevent patrons from watching more than one movie on a single ticket. Once people have shown their tickets to the attendant at the entrance to the multiplex, there are generally no further checks. Having seen the film they came to see, patrons are thus free to see a second or even a third film at no additional charge. In contrast, tickets are checked carefully at the entrance to each screening hall in most Asian cineplexes. Why this difference?

A plausible explanation begins with the observation, discussed in the preceding example, that film showings typically have many empty seats in American theaters but are usually sold out in Asian theaters. Thus if American moviegoers were to see a second film without buying a second ticket, they would not prevent anyone else from seeing that film. In contrast, if people were to see a second film without buying a second ticket in an Asian theater, they would displace others from seeing it.

The benefit of preventing people from seeing more than one movie on a single ticket is therefore larger in crowded Asian theaters than in half-empty American ones. And since hiring ticket checkers for each separate screen is costly, Asian theater managers have greater incentive to follow through.

It is also possible that American theater managers are boosting their revenue from ticket sales by not enforcing the one film per ticket rule. Despite the fact that there is no separate ticket check in each hall in American movie houses, most American moviegoers see only a single film per visit. The question is whether the few patrons who choose to see more than one film would have bought a ticket at all except for the fact that doing so enabled them to see multiple films. If not, then not enforcing the one film per ticket rule boosts total ticket revenues.

In other words, the lack of an enforcement policy may be just another form of price discrimination. People willing to violate the unenforced one film per ticket rule are likely to be more price sensitive, on average, than others. The lack of an enforcement policy may thus function as a simple hurdle that enables theater managers to make these patrons eligible for discounts without cutting prices for everyone.

In any event, the extra revenue from extra visits to the concession stand is likely to nullify any losses from lost ticket sales attributable to multifilm viewers.

As the next example illustrates, other interesting international differences may spring from differences in the opportunity costs of pursuing various occupations.

Why have U.S. men been so unsuccessful in international soccer competition? And why have U.S. women fared so much better? *(Dave Decker)*

Over the past century, the United States has consistently been among the leaders in total Olympic gold medalists, male or female. In recent years, American women have been remarkably successful in world soccer competition. But the country's men's soccer teams have been notably less successful. Why this difference?

Before the 1960s, soccer was rarely played in American schools, much less at the professional level. While the game has made considerable inroads in the United States since then, it remains a second-tier sport. Football, baseball, basketball, and hockey, which have long paid professional athletes annual salaries in seven figures, compete vigorously for the attention of the most talented young athletes. Consequently American soccer has always had a limited talent pool to draw from.

In contrast, soccer is the dominant men's sport elsewhere in the world. In most countries, every talented young athlete dreams of becoming a soccer star. American men's soccer teams find international competition challenging because their rivals from other countries have had their pick of the very best aspiring athletes.

American women find themselves in a more favorable situation internationally, since in many other countries, women's participation in athletics is limited. In the United States, however, Title IX legislation requires parity in school athletic program spending for boys and girls. And in the absence of highly paid professional sports leagues for women in the United States, the most talented female athletes have not been bid away by other sports.

ALTHOUGH MANY INTERESTING international differences in behavior are a consequence of prices and incomes, some are more plausibly attributed to differences in economic policy choices.

Why is the unemployment rate so much higher in Germany than in the United States? *(Martin Mehalchin)*

Although the unemployment rate in most countries varies from month to month, there are also persistent differences across countries. The unemployment rate in the United States, for example, is consistently lower than that of most European countries. In September 2006, it was 4.6 percent in the United States but 8.7 percent in Germany. Why is the German unemployment rate so much higher?

One way to approach this question is to examine differences in the individual costs and benefits of being unemployed in the two countries. Compared to the citizens of most other developed countries, Americans rely more heavily on employment to meet their basic economic needs. Health insurance, for example, is provided primarily by employers in the United States, but is provided by the government in Germany. And although the United States has an unemployment insurance system that helps support workers who lose their jobs, the compensation payments are smaller and the benefits expire more quickly than in Germany. Social welfare payments to low-income people are also more generous and less restrictive in Germany than in the United States.

Most Germans, like most Americans, have steady jobs and appear to take satisfaction in them. But conditions for those without jobs differ sharply in the two countries. Americans without jobs have difficulty making ends meet. In contrast, the unemployed in Germany can qualify for government support that will satisfy their basic needs indefinitely.

In short, the opportunity cost of not working is lower in Germany than in the United States, and this difference helps explain why unemployed Germans can afford to be more patient and selective in their search for the right job.

Why do consumers in the United States pay more than double the world price for sugar? *(Thomas Pugel)*

In 2005 Americans paid an average of twenty-two cents a pound for raw sugar, while the average price on the world market was only ten cents. What explains this huge price gap?

The short answer is that the United States imposes a tariff of more than 100 percent on imported sugar. But that begs the question of why legislators in Congress would enact policies that cost their constituents some $2 billion each year. A plausible answer begins with the observation that the incentives facing voters are different from those facing domestic sugar producers.

Because the typical family spends only a small fraction of 1 percent of its income on sugar, few voters would ever take the trouble to complain to their elected representatives about the high price of sugar. Indeed, most voters probably do not even realize that a tariff on imported sugar exists.

For sugar producers, the incentives are very different. For example, the sugar tariff was estimated to increase the annual profits of one large producer in Florida by some $65 million. With that much at stake, producers not only write letters but hire skilled lobbyists to argue their case. More important, they make substantial campaign contributions to legislators who support the sugar tariff.

Producers gain less than half the cost imposed on American consumers, yet political support for tariff repeal remains elusive because the benefits of the tariff are concentrated and its costs highly diffuse.

Why are automobile engines much smaller in Europe than in the United States?

BMW sells its 5 Series sedan all around the globe. In Europe, many drivers choose the 1.6 liter engine with four cylinders, but the smallest option available in the United States is a three-liter, six-cylinder engine. In general, cars sold in Europe have substantially smaller engine displacement and fewer cylinders than cars sold in the United States. Why do Europeans buy cars with smaller engines?

Smaller engines in European markets:
A consequence of higher gasoline taxes?

Drawing by Mick Stevens.

Some might think that the crowded European roads render high-performance automobiles less useful in Europe than in the United States. Yet there are no speed limits on many European freeways, where it is common to see Porsche and Ferrari drivers speed by at 150 miles per hour.

Those drivers, of course, are people for whom money is of little concern. Average Europeans are more likely than average Americans to shun cars with large engines because gasoline is heavily taxed in Europe. In recent years, for example, the average price of a gallon of gasoline, including all taxes, has been almost twice as high in Europe as in the United States. Another factor is that some European countries tax automobiles partly on the basis of their engine displacement.

Europeans choose smaller engines not because they don't like fast cars but because the financial penalty for large engines is so high.

Why do new luxury cars account for a higher proportion of automobiles sold in Singapore than in the United States? *(Jacqueline Chien)*

The average income in Singapore is about one-third smaller than in the United States, and the income distributions in the two countries are strikingly similar. Yet BMW, Mercedes, and other luxury manufacturers enjoy a much higher market share in Singapore. Why are Singaporeans more likely to buy luxury cars?

Because of Singapore's high population density, the country's government has taken aggressive steps to curb pollution and congestion. For example, it has built an efficient system of public transportation and imposed substantial license fees on automobiles. For present purposes, three features of Singapore auto license fees are important. First, they are extremely high, well in excess of the pretax price of even the most expensive luxury car. Second, large components of them do not depend on the price of the car purchased. They are the same for a BMW 745i as for a Honda Civic, even though the BMW costs five times as much as the Civic. And third, the fees are much higher for older vehicles than for newer ones, in recognition of the fact that automobile pollution control technology has been steadily improving. By making the fees higher for dirtier, older vehicles, the government thus gives motorists an incentive to purchase newer, cleaner ones.

These license fees make car ownership so expensive that a far smaller proportion of people own cars in Singapore than in the United States. Low- and middle-income Singaporeans typically rely exclusively on public transportation, with car ownership restricted to the relatively wealthy. Another consequence is that while buyers in America often pay five times as much for a luxury car as for an economy car, the corresponding multiple in Singapore is typically less than three.

In sum, the fact that car license fees rise steeply for older vehicles explains why the proportion of new cars on the road in Singapore is higher than the corresponding proportion in the United States. And the fact that high fees restrict car ownership to the wealthy, combined with the fact that the price (inclusive of license fees) of luxury cars is low relative to the price of economy cars in Singapore, explains why the proportion of new luxury cars on the road is much higher in Singapore.

Why are pedestrians fined for jaywalking in Rome but not in New York?
(Jose Weiss)

As anyone who has ever visited Manhattan can attest, pedestrians in the Big Apple pay little heed to traffic lights. If even the briefest opening presents itself, they will cross the street even when oncoming traffic has a green light. And they do this in full view of policemen on foot patrol, secure in the knowledge that although jaywalking is formally prohibited by law, violators are almost never ticketed. In Rome, by contrast, police routinely ticket jaywalkers, which has made the offense relatively rare in that city. Why this difference?

If the task were to explain why jaywalkers are ticketed in Berlin, a plausible answer might be that Germans are renowned for enforcing rules of all sort. But this is seldom said of Italians.

There is, however, one salient difference between traffic conditions in New York and Rome that may help explain their different enforcement policies. In New York, virtually all street traffic consists of cars and trucks. If a jaywalker steps in front of a car or truck, he is likely to be severely injured or killed, but unlikely to cause physical injury to the vehicle's driver. In contrast, much of Rome's street traffic consists of bicycles and motor scooters. A jaywalker in Rome thus incurs a somewhat smaller risk to his own life than one in New York but is more likely to jeopardize the lives of others.

Ultimately the difference in ticketing practices appears to be an indirect consequence of tax policy differences. High gasoline and vehicle taxes in Italy explain why bicycles and scooters are more prevalent in Rome than in New York, and thus why jaywalking laws are taken more seriously.

THE NEXT EXAMPLE calls attention to an interesting difference in how seemingly similar products are marketed in different countries.

Why does the DVD format used in the United States differ from those used in Europe and elsewhere, while CD formats are the same in all countries?
(Valerie Bouchereau)

If a French tourist visiting relatives in New York brings a DVD purchased in Paris as a gift, they will quickly discover that American DVD players cannot read it. Similarly, if she buys a DVD in New York, she will be disappointed to discover that her French DVD player cannot read the American disc. With CDs, however, such problems never arise. A CD purchased anywhere on the planet can be read easily by CD players sold in every country. Why do DVD sellers, but not CD sellers, employ multiple formats?

A plausible answer is suggested by the observation that movie studios have two products to sell to the mass market—theater screenings and DVDs—whereas music companies have only one, CDs. What these three products have in common is the fact that the marginal cost of serving an additional customer is very low. For most films shown in theaters, for example, there are additional empty seats for at least some screenings. And once a film or music album is produced, the cost of burning an extra CD or DVD is only pennies. The fact that movie studios have two products to sell gives them an incentive to adopt a distinctive marketing strategy.

Every seller's goal is to get buyers to pay as much as possible for its product. As noted earlier, a useful means to that end is to offer it at a discount, but only if customers are willing to jump some hurdle. One particularly useful hurdle for film studios is to charge high prices for movies shown in theaters and lower prices for DVDs released several months later. Thus it might cost a family of four $40 to see a film at a theater just after its release, whereas those who are willing to wait can rent the DVD for $3 and watch it at home. Releasing the DVD at the same time the film is released in theaters would compromise the sale of expensive theater tickets.

Studios typically stagger a film's release date across different major international markets so that actors can do local publicity tours just before its release in each market. Thus a studio might release a film in the United States in September, Europe in February, and Asia in June. If

DVD formats were the same around the world and the DVD were released in the United States in February, consumers in Europe and Japan could rent it from a shop that bought it on amazon.com, thereby getting to see it as quickly as their theatergoing neighbors without having to pay the higher prices. Having different DVD formats for different countries is an attempt to prevent this.

It might seem that music companies would face similar incentives. After all, staggering CD release dates across international markets would enable musicians to tour in those countries just as their CDs were being released. But whereas movie companies earn revenue from both theater and DVD sales, recording labels earn revenue only from CD sales. When a band goes on tour, the money from concert ticket sales goes directly to the musicians, not their recording labels. Music companies thus have little to gain by trying to keep CDs from traveling freely across national borders.

SOME INTERNATIONAL DIFFERENCES spring not from differences in incomes, prices, or economic policies, but rather from differences in incentives originating in different social customs.

Why do Japanese couples spend more on wedding parties than their American counterparts? *(Tsutomu Ito)*

On average, Japanese couples spend more than twice as much to celebrate their weddings as American couples do. Although spending per guest is higher in Japan than in the United States, the main explanation for the cost difference is that Japanese couples tend to invite more guests. Why are Japanese wedding parties so much larger?

Japanese couples commonly celebrate their weddings with an extended network of coworkers, employers, and other members of the community. Local politicians are often invited even if they do not know the bridal couple personally. Guest lists frequently total from three hundred to five hundred people, even at weddings of middle-income couples.

Japanese couples cast such a broad net in part because their society relies heavily on informal social and business networks. A strong commitment to social harmony *(wa)* is an essential ingredient in maintaining

Drawing by Mick Stevens.

Large weddings: Investments in business and social networks?

one's position in these networks. Failing to invite someone to a wedding who might have expected to be invited risks a social rupture that jeopardizes one's standing. Expansive Japanese wedding guest lists may thus be seen as an investment in maintaining important social and business networks. Such networks also exist in the United States but are generally far less important than in Japan.

9

Psychology Meets Economics

lthough economists often assume that people are rational and narrowly self-interested, the emerging field of behavioral economics challenges these assumptions. We leave tips, for example, even in restaurants we will never visit again, and our decisions are often influenced by information that is manifestly irrelevant.

Much of the pioneering work in behavioral economics was done by two Israeli psychologists, Daniel Kahneman and the late Amos Tversky. In one experiment, they asked a sample of undergraduate students to estimate the percentage of African nations that are members of the United Nations. Most students had no idea, but their task was to come up with a number. The twist in the experiment was that before being asked the question, students were told to spin a random number wheel that was equally likely to land on any number between one and one hundred. As the students surely understood, the number that came up could have no logical bearing on the answer to the question. Yet students who got a ten or less on the wheel reported an average estimate of 25 percent, while those who got sixty-five or more reported an average estimate of 45 percent.

Much of behavioral economics has focused on these kinds of cognitive errors. As the first several examples in this chapter illustrate, people sometimes rely on the wrong information when making decisions; other times they draw faulty inferences from the correct information.

Why does Cornell University have a reputation for a high suicide rate among students when its actual rate is well below the national average for university students? (Jason Tagler)

Cornell University has a suicide rate of 4.3 per 100,000 student-years, which is less than half the national average for university students. Yet Cornell has long been perceived as having an unusually high suicide rate. Why this discrepancy?

According to Kahneman and Tversky, people use heuristics, or crude rule of thumb reasoning, to make estimates about events in the world. For example, when people try to estimate the frequency of a given event, they often use the availability heuristic, which holds that an event is more frequent if examples of it are easier to remember. On average, the availability heuristic works reasonably well because it is easier to recall examples of events that happen more frequently.

But frequency is not the only factor that makes us remember events. Another is salience, and here we find a plausible explanation for why people overestimate Cornell's suicide rate. At other universities, students typically use relatively undramatic means to kill themselves, such as overdosing on sleeping pills. But Cornell is bordered on two sides by deep glaciated gorges, and many Cornell suicides occur when students jump from the bridges that span these gorges. Traffic surrounding the bridges may be tied up for hours while recovery teams rappel into the gorges to bring out the body. So when people ask themselves whether Cornell has a high suicide rate, they tend to answer affirmatively because it is so easy to summon examples from memory. Unless they knew the victim, most people do not remember examples of suicide by drug overdose.

Why do real estate agents often show clients two nearly identical houses, even though one is both cheaper and in better condition than the other?

A home buyer is having a hard time making up his mind between two houses. One is a Greek Revival farmhouse in impeccable condition listed at $300,000, the other a recently remodeled Victorian townhouse listed at $280,000. He is leaning toward the Victorian townhouse. His real estate agent then makes an appointment for him to see a second Greek Revival farmhouse. This one is in slightly worse condition than the first and is listed at $320,000. As the two are driving back from this visit, the home buyer announces his intention to buy the first Greek Revival farmhouse. What led the real estate agent to think it would be a good idea to show him the second one?

This episode evokes the story of a man who asks the waitress at a lunch counter what kinds of sandwiches are on the menu. "We have chicken salad and roast beef," replies the waitress, whereupon the diner orders roast beef. The waitress then adds, "I forgot, we also have tuna," to which the diner responds, "In that case, I'll have chicken salad."

In switching his order, the diner has violated a fundamental axiom of rational choice theory, which is that adding an inferior element to a list of options should not alter the option chosen. The diner's initial choice implied a preference for roast beef over chicken salad, a preference that should not have been altered by the addition of tuna to the list of options.

As Itamar Simonson and Amos Tversky have shown, however, such preference reversals are actually common. What seems to be going on is that people often have trouble choosing between two options that are difficult to compare. Each has attractive attributes, and people are reluctant to choose one for fear that they may later regret not taking the other. In such situations, Simonson and Tversky argue, the introduction of a seemingly irrelevant new option can have a profound effect.

The real estate agent's client could not choose between the first Greek Revival farmhouse and the Victorian townhouse. But he experienced no such anxiety when comparing the first farmhouse to the second, because the second was inferior in both quality and price. The first farmhouse's easy victory in this comparison creates a halo effect that carries over to the comparison with the Victorian townhouse.

According to traditional rational choice theory, showing the second farmhouse should have been a complete waste of time. In practice, however, such tactics are often effective.

Why does Victoria's Secret offer multimillion-dollar jewel-studded bras that no one ever buys? *(Stephanie Wenstrup)*

For the past decade, Victoria's Secret has highlighted one particularly expensive gift in each year's Christmas catalog. The series was launched in 1996, when Claudia Schiffer modeled the company's $1 million diamond-studded Miracle Bra. The following year, Tyra Banks arrived in an armored car at the showroom of Harry Winston jewelers on Fifth Avenue in New York wearing the 1997 Victoria's Secret supergift, a $3 million bra ornamented with sapphires and diamonds. The 2006 entry, crafted by Hearts On Fire and modeled by Karolina Kurkova, was listed at $6.5 million. Given that no one has ever purchased any of these bejeweled bras, why does Victoria's Secret continue to offer them?

The company probably never expected to sell these bras. Yet offering them may be a winning tactic because of its effect on sales of other offerings. The bejeweled bras continue to attract media interest, bringing the Victoria's Secret brand to the attention of potential customers.

Photo courtesy Hearts on Fire.

*The 2006 Victoria's Secret Diamond Fantasy Bra
by Hearts On Fire: $6.5 Million.*

The company is clearly conscious of this benefit, as evidenced by its recognition that each new garment will attract attention only if it is more spectacular than earlier offerings. If the garments do not sell, it is of little consequence since the jewels can easily be recycled.

But perhaps the most important benefit of the bejeweled bra offerings is one that economists often overlook—their mere presence in the catalog shifts the frame of reference that defines appropriate spending for a gift. By planting the thought that others are spending millions, Victoria's Secret makes the idea of spending several hundred dollars seem less preposterous. It is easy to imagine that an eager husband, having just seen the $6.5 million Fantasy Bra, might hand over $298 for the company's Chantal Thomass Pinstripe Merrywidow and think what a thrifty shopper he'd been.

Why are some brands of ice cream sold only in pint containers, while others are sold only in half gallons? *(Pattie Koontz, Monica Devine)*

Local supermarkets typically carry multiple brands and flavors of ice cream. But fans of a particular brand often cannot find it in the size they prefer. For example, Ithaca's largest supermarket carries Breyer's ice cream in multiple flavors, but only in half gallon containers. The store also carries Ben & Jerry's ice cream in multiple flavors, but only in pint containers. Why this difference?

Ben & Jerry's is widely perceived as a premium ice cream, in part because the company uses expensive ingredients and processing methods, and in part because of its reputation for environmentally sensitive procurement practices and humane employee relations programs. Because its costs are higher, it must charge higher prices. A pint container of Ben & Jerry's New York super fudge chunk sells for $3.69, for example, a price that would translate to $14.76 a half gallon. A half gallon of Breyers mint chocolate chip, by contrast, sells for only $4.99.

Evidence suggests that consumers are sensitive not only to the price per ounce but to the total product price. When premium ice creams first entered the market, consumers were accustomed to paying relatively low prices for ice cream sold in half gallon containers. They realize that Ben & Jerry's tastes better and is more expensive than most other brands of ice cream. Even so, many would be shocked to see a $15 price tag on a container of ice cream. By making its flavors available only in pint containers, Ben & Jerry's deftly sidestepped the problem of sticker shock. And people who want to purchase larger quantities always have the option of buying more than one pint.

PRIMARILY FOR SIMPLICITY'S SAKE, economic models traditionally assume that people are self-interested in the narrow sense of the term. Obviously self-interest is an important human motive, but people are driven by other motives as well. The narrow pursuit of self-interest cannot explain, for example, why people donate anonymously to charities or vote in presidential elections. Behavioral economics tells us we must employ a more nuanced view of human motivation if we want to understand the actual economic choices people make.

Ethical concerns often leave a clear imprint on market transactions, although not always in expected ways.

Why is it impossible to find a hotel room in the host city on Super Bowl weekend? *(Richard Thaler, Harry Chan)*

The Super Bowl is the top entertainment event in the United States each year. And each year in the host city it is all but impossible to find a hotel room on the Saturday before Sunday's game. Some have speculated that the market-clearing price for rooms that Saturday might be as high as several thousand dollars. Although some hotels do post higher rates for Super Bowl weekend, almost none charges more than $500 per room, and most charge considerably less. Why don't hotels in the host city simply raise their prices?

Although their failure to do so seems to be a clear example of leaving cash on the table, other explanations are possible. One is that excess demand catches hotels by surprise, as sometimes happens when a popular new car model sells out unexpectedly at the manufacturer's suggested retail price. This explanation is clearly implausible in the case of pre-Super Bowl hotel rooms. Hoteliers are virtually certain of excess demand for these rooms. After all, it happens every year, and the venue (unlike that of the World Series) is determined far in advance.

A more promising explanation is that hotels may be reluctant to antagonize their customers by charging what are perceived to be unfair prices. But why should a hotel care about such reactions? If people think the market-clearing price is too high for their taste, they have the option of refusing to pay it. And given the predictably long queues of frustrated fans unable to find rooms, hotels could be fairly confident of selling out even if some people found their high prices unfair.

Still, it might be a risky strategy to charge what the market would bear on such occasions. Many consumers might reluctantly pay the market-clearing price but feel a lingering resentment at having been charged so much. Such reactions matter, especially to the proprietors of hotel chains, who have rooms to sell not just on the Saturday night before the Super Bowl but on hundreds of other nights in hundreds of other cities. Someone who feels Hilton gouged him on Super Bowl weekend in Miami in February may be less likely to choose Hilton when he travels to St. Louis on business in March.

This explanation is consistent with pricing anomalies in other domains. Popular restaurants, for example, know they will have more demand for tables on Saturday night than they can possibly accommodate at their regular menu prices. But restaurateurs have tables to fill on other nights of the week as well. And they seem concerned that if customers feel they've been taken advantage of on Saturdays, they'll be more likely to dine elsewhere on Tuesdays.

Why are more firms outsourcing custodial work?

Every firm must decide which services to perform for itself and which to delegate to outside contractors. As Chapter 3's example about hiring outside management consultants suggested, a firm is more likely to hire its own employees to provide services that occur on a steady, ongoing basis and more likely to hire outside contractors for services required only intermittently. Contrary to this pattern, however, recent years have seen a large increase in outsourcing of custodial services, which would appear to be an example of the first type. Why incur the overhead costs of hiring outside companies to provide daily custodial services?

One possible explanation is suggested by studies showing that employees performing a given task earn higher salaries when they work for more prosperous employers. An economically prosperous firm might thus be viewed as unfair if it hired custodial workers at the minimum wage and offered meager employee benefits. But the same custodians might be willing to accept employment on those terms with an outside contractor whose own economic circumstances were relatively modest. Thus a wage of $6 an hour might seem fair if paid by a struggling independent contractor but extremely unfair if paid by IBM or Google. The growth of income disparities that has occurred in recent decades can only have increased the salience of such concerns.

Why are people more likely to return cash to a store when given too much change by a cashier than to return a piece of merchandise for which they were not charged? (Bradley Stanczak)

In response to an informal survey, more than 90 percent of respondents said they would return $20 to the store if given that amount of excess change by a Target cashier. But only 10 percent of respondents said they would return a $20 lampshade to Target if the cashier had neglected to charge them for it. Why are people more likely to be honest in one case than the other?

As philosophers have long emphasized, honest behavior is motivated not just by fear of punishment but also by moral sentiments such as sympathy and guilt. The customer could keep either the excess change or the lampshade with no fear of punishment. But the two actions are likely to trigger a different mix of moral sentiments.

If the customer keeps the cash, the cashier's register will show a $20 shortfall at the end of the day, which the cashier will have to pay out of her own pocket. Cashiers generally earn modest salaries, and the thought of being responsible for someone they have dealt with face-to-face having to sacrifice one-third of her daily pay triggers an uneasy response in most consumers.

But if the consumer does not report failure to be charged for a $20 lampshade, the consequence will be to lower Target's annual profits by that amount. As a percentage of the company's total profit, this is a vanishingly small loss, and the burden will be divided among shareholders the consumer has never seen and imagines to be wealthy. No moral theory would count those facts as valid reasons for keeping the lampshade. But they do help explain why the moral sentiments that support honest behavior are more likely to be triggered when a consumer is given too much change.

IN TRADITIONAL ECONOMIC MODELS, money is perfectly fungible. Because it can be used for whatever purpose the holder wishes, cash rewards are thought to trump other rewards of equivalent value. Yet people often seem to prefer rewards in kind. Behavioral economics has helped us better understand such preferences by focusing our attention on a variety of factors that constrain people from spending their cash as they see fit.

Why did a New Jersey telecommunications company give its employees a "free" BMW rather than an equivalent bonus in cash?

When a business cannot hire and retain enough qualified workers, economics suggests a ready solution: offer higher salaries. But some employers appear to have adopted a different strategy. For example, Arcnet, a wireless telecommunications company in Holmdel, New Jersey, hoped to slash its recruiting and training costs by offering a "free" BMW sedan to every employee with at least one year of service. Several other companies have reported success with similar offers.

The cars are not really free, of course. Each costs about $9,000 a year in leasing and insurance fees. Employees who get one must declare that amount as additional income to the Internal Revenue Service. So we're left with a puzzle: if the company had given not the car but an additional $9,000 a year in salary, no one should have been worse off, and at least some should have been better off.

After all, any worker who really wanted a BMW could have spent the extra cash to lease one. And although the BMW is a fine car, those who happen not to want one would have come out ahead by having $9,000 a year extra to spend on other things. Why, then, do employers give cars instead of cash?

Essentially the same question is raised by ordinary gift exchanges among family and friends. Why give your cousin a necktie he might never wear when you know you could trust him to spend the same money on something he really wants?

Some would answer that giving cash is just too easy and is hence a less effective way of demonstrating affection than taking the time and trouble to shop for a gift. That explanation might work for small gifts, but it's surely a stretch for luxury cars.

A more promising tack has been suggested by the economist Richard Thaler, who observes that the best gifts are often things we're reluctant to buy for ourselves. Why, he asks, is a man happy when his wife gives him a $1,000 set of titanium golf clubs paid for out of their joint checking account? Perhaps he really wanted those clubs but couldn't justify spending so much. Having someone else make the choice allows him to enjoy his new clubs guilt free.

One attraction of this way of thinking about gift giving is the plausibility of the advice it suggests for gift givers. Consider this thought experiment: Among each of the following pairs of items costing the same amounts, which item would be the more suitable gift for a close friend?

- $20 worth of macadamia nuts (1 pound) or $20 worth of peanuts (10 pounds)?

- A $75 gift certificate for Spago (one lunch) or a $75 gift certificate for McDonald's (15 lunches)?

- $30 worth of wild rice (4 pounds) or $30 worth of Uncle Ben's converted rice (50 pounds)?

- A $60 bottle of Mondavi Reserve Cabernet (750 ml) or $60 worth of Cribari red (10 gallons)?

Most people consider the first item in each pair the safer choice.

The same logic may explain why Arcnet and other employers in the fast lane are giving away BMWs. Perhaps you'd find it awkward to tell your Depression-era parents that you'd bought a car costing twice as much as a Toyota Camry. Or you might worry that your neighbors would think you were putting on airs. Or perhaps you've always wanted a BMW but your spouse insists on remodeling the kitchen instead.

A gift car from your employer wipes away such concerns. From the company's perspective, an added advantage is that offering a luxury car to all long-term employees would kindle fewer resentments than the alternative strategy—also becoming more common—of offering cash signing bonuses to new recruits.

Is the American labor market headed for a full-fledged barter system? Not likely, since the Arcnet strategy would make little sense for many employers. Burger King franchise owners, for example, probably won't dangle used Ford Escorts the next time they find themselves short of counter help. They and other employers of unskilled labor are more likely to stick with the time-honored strategy of paying higher wages.

But in-kind compensation is likely to spread among employers of the most highly skilled workers. It is these employers who face consistent labor shortages, and it's the people they are trying to hire and retain who are responsive to the new luxury offerings.

As the trend unfolds, the gifts are likely to change. The strategy depends on the gift's ability to generate excitement, which always and everywhere depends on context. Most readers were astonished when the young lawyer in John Grisham's 1991 novel *The Firm* was given a new BMW as a signing bonus, and the same tactic attracts media attention even today. As more and more companies adopt it, however, it will inevitably lose its punch, and employers will have to raise the stakes. Can anyone doubt that talented consultants and investment bankers will eventually snub any employer who dares offer less than a Porsche 911 or a time-share in Los Cabos?

TRADITIONAL ECONOMIC MODELS assume people have well-defined goals that they pursue efficiently. Recent work in behavioral economics, however, has shown that people's choices are shaped to a considerable extent by a psychological drive to construct and preserve individual and group identity. This insight helps explain a variety of choices whose logic might not be immediately apparent from traditional economic models.

Why don't more people wear Velcro shoes? *(Adam Goldstein)*

Learning to tie one's shoelaces was a childhood rite of passage long before Swiss inventor George de Mestral obtained a patent for Velcro in 1955. Ever since then, Velcro has been replacing zippers, hooks, laces, and other traditional fastening methods in a host of applications. As a method of fastening shoes, Velcro offers clear advantages over laces. Laces can become untied, for example, causing people to trip and fall. And fastening shoes with Velcro is much quicker and easier than tying a pair of laces. But although it once seemed that Velcro might drive laces from the marketplace, the proportion of adults who wear shoes with Velcro fasteners remains small. Why have shoelaces survived?

From the beginning, the most popular applications of Velcro in the shoe industry have been in shoes for children as well as the elderly and infirm. Velcro's popularity in children's shoes is explained by the fact that many of the youngest children have not yet learned to tie shoelaces. Shoes with Velcro fasteners afford these children—and their parents—a welcome measure of independence. Among the elderly, Velcro is popular for medical reasons. Some older people have difficulty bending down to tie their shoes, for example, while others have difficulty because of arthritic fingers.

The upshot is that Velcro fasteners on footwear are associated in the public mind with incompetence and fragility. Even though shoes that fasten with Velcro are in many ways more serviceable than those that fasten with laces, shoelaces are unlikely to disappear anytime soon.

Why did kamikaze pilots wear helmets? *(Chanan Glambosky)*

On the heels of significant military setbacks in 1944, the Japanese military launched a campaign of kamikaze attacks in which pilots attempted to crash their planes into American warships. Their planes were heavily laden with explosives, so a crash meant almost certain death for the pilot. Why, then, did these pilots wear helmets?

One reason is that in at least some instances, kamikaze pilots survived their missions. Another is that planes commonly experienced severe turbulence before reaching their targets, and in these cases

The Kamikaze pilot's helmet: A symbol of identity?

Drawing by Mick Stevens.

Japanese military commanders had clear reasons for wanting their pilots to be adequately protected. Perhaps even more important, the aviator's helmet had become emblematic of what it meant to be a pilot. Kamikaze pilots were pilots, and all pilots wear helmets.

But the most compelling explanation for why kamikaze pilots wore helmets is that it was not the express intention that these pilots commit suicide. Their charge was to destroy their targets by any means necessary. Often that meant flying into such heavy antiaircraft fire that survival became unlikely. Other times there was no way to deliver their lethal explosives except by flying directly into the target. But the hope was that the pilots would return safely, even though the expectation was that most would not.

Why does women's clothing at U.S. retailers come in numbered sizes (2–14), as opposed to the measured sizes in which men's clothing is available? (Salli Schwartz, Sarah Katt)

When a man with a thirty-four-inch waist and a thirty-three-inch inseam shopped for pants in 1960, he looked for a pair on which the size label read "W: 34, L: 33." If an identical man shopped for pants today, he would follow exactly the same strategy. In contrast, the size labels on women's garments—typically, even numbers that range from 0 to 18—bear no obvious relationship to a woman's actual measurements. And the number that would have fit a woman of a given size in 1960 will generally be found on a garment that would be far too big for the same size woman today. Why are women's sizes so uninformative?

In 1958 the Department of Commerce published a commercial standard for women's clothing sizes. But retailers quickly discovered that they could boost their sales by placing smaller numbers on garments of any given phyical size, a practice that became known as vanity sizing. Departures from the published standard became increasingly widespread, leading the Department of Commerce to abandon it in 1983. Today no manufacturer that refused to practice vanity sizing could hope to remain in business. Many women, it seems, prefer garments bearing smaller size numbers because such garments create the illusion of being more svelte.

But even as their size numbers have been going down, women have been getting bigger. The average American woman today weighs about twenty-five pounds more than her counterpart in 1960. Thus the deflation of women's size numbers has roughly offset the increase in their actual sizes. As any woman who has shopped in a vintage clothing store can attest, a size 8 from 1960 is much smaller than a size 8 today. But today's size 8 fits the average woman today, just as size 8 fit the average woman in 1960.

Men have also been getting bigger over time. Why haven't men's clothing manufacturers engaged in similar vanity sizing? In light of the growing number of men availing themselves of hair transplants and cosmetic surgery, the answer cannot be that men are not vain. The objective measurement scheme used to label men's clothing may simply be less amenable to manipulation by manufacturers.

Why do most department stores place men's fashions on the lower floors and women's fashions on the higher floors? *(Rima Sawaya)*

In Macy's and Bloomingdale's, most of the men's clothing is located on the ground floor, whereas most of the women's clothing is located on the top three floors. With few exceptions, the same pattern holds in department stores around the world. Why do many stores provide easier access to the men's department?

Although most men and women want to appear well dressed in public, appearance is often said to weigh more heavily in women's identity construction. In any event, the fact that women spend more than twice as much as men on clothing suggests that women take shopping for clothing more seriously than men do. Accordingly, few women are likely to be deterred from reaching the women's clothing department by the mere fact that they must ride an elevator to get there.

In contrast, even a minimal obstacle would prevent many men from reaching the men's clothing department. Most feel they don't really need a new suit, after all, and if shopping for one were slightly less convenient, many would postpone the errand.

An additional advantage of putting men's clothing on the ground floor is that wives often purchase clothing for their husbands. A woman passing through men's wear might well pick up an additional pair of socks or a couple of dress shirts for her husband. Men rarely buy clothing for their wives, so stores would gain little if the layout were reversed.

Why do baseball managers wear uniforms? *(Andrew Toburen)*

Baseball is the only major professional sport in which team managers wear the same uniforms as their players. Basketball coaches in the NBA typically wear suits and ties, as do hockey coaches in the NHL. NFL football coaches typically wear parkas and baseball caps on the sidelines. Why are baseball managers the only ones to wear uniforms?

As anyone who recalls the spectacle of former Chicago Cubs manager Don Zimmer limping out to the mound to confer with one of his pitchers, the answer does not seem to be that baseball uniforms flatter the male form in late middle age.

A more plausible explanation for uniforms on baseball managers begins with the observation that baseball was an organized professional sport long before basketball, football, and hockey were. With no precedent about what managers should wear, there was no presumption that

Drawing by Mick Stevens.

Coaches in uniform: Why only in baseball?

managers would dress differently from players, and early uniforms were baggy enough to conceal a form well past its prime.

Moreover, because baseball is a not an aerobically demanding sport, it is not uncommon even for players to be noticeably overweight. An out-of-shape manager in a baseball uniform would thus have been less conspicuous than an out-of-shape coach in a basketball uniform. In the same vein, baseball differs from other sports in that managers frequently enter the field of play, as when they walk to the mound to make pitching changes. A man in a business suit might look jarringly out of place in such situations. Finally, a number of managers were simultaneously active players in baseball's early days, so wearing uniforms would have made perfect sense for them.

But perhaps the simplest way to understand why managers in the other major sports don't wear uniforms is to imagine how ridiculous they would look if they did. For example, picture Jeff Van Gundy on the Houston Rockets sideline dressed in shorts and a tank top, or Bill Parcells in shoulder pads and skin-tight Cowboys knickers, or Ted Nolan in full New York Islanders regalia. Baseball uniforms may not flatter the middle-age male physique, but baseball managers in uniform are a far less comical spectacle than uniformed managers would be in the other major sports.

The next example illustrates a principle that business owners have long grasped but many economists are just beginning to appreciate—a little common sense about human psychology gives rise to marketing strategies that can substantially boost a business's earnings.

Why does Target promote prescription drugs sold at its in-store pharmacies so heavily? *(Kate Rubinstein)*

Target Stores offer a broad range of products, many of which they advertise and promote. But they give particular emphasis to prescription drugs from their in-store pharmacies. When Target opens a new store, for example, it sends out a high volume of promotional coupons, many of which are linked to its pharmacy. ("Transfer your prescription to the Target pharmacy and get $10 off your next purchase.") Why this emphasis?

If customers who present a prescription to a pharmacist are lucky, their wait for it may be as short as five minutes. But if the drug counter is busy, it may be twenty minutes or more. Anticipating this wait, rational consumers would bring something to read. But Target executives seem to realize that most consumers don't think that far ahead. They also know that such customers are unlikely to sit idly while waiting for their prescriptions. With aisles full of attractive merchandise close at hand, the typical consumer chooses to browse the store. Luring additional customers to its pharmacy is thus an effective way of getting them to make other purchases as well.

Several examples in Chapter 6 illustrated how laws and regulations reconcile conflicts between individuals and groups. Another strategy is for groups to embrace social norms that attempt to bring individual and group incentives into balance. When more people are waiting for the next bus than there are seats on that bus, tense scuffles often erupt as they jockey for position. Yet no matter how aggressively people behave, the number of available seats remains the same. The British Commonwealth countries have solved this problem by embracing a norm under which the first arrivals in the queue are acknowledged by all to have first claim on the available seats.

Such norms promote efficiency and social harmony. But as this chapter's final example illustrates, the first-come, first-served norm sometimes has undesired consequences.

Why does social courtesy sometimes lead to inefficient outcomes on one-lane bridges? *(Mario Caporicci, Scott Magrath)*

Ithaca, New York, has several one-lane bridges. Over the years, a first-come, first-served social norm has developed that governs the order of passage across these bridges. Under this norm, no car is supposed to enter the bridge if another car was already waiting on the other side. The ostensible purpose of this norm is to prevent a steady stream of traffic from one direction from blocking access to the bridge for extended periods. As noted, in many, perhaps even most, instances, social norms that urge self-restraint bring about more efficient outcomes than would otherwise be possible. But in this instance, attempts to be courteous often make for less efficient outcomes. Why would motorists follow such a norm?

To begin, imagine what traffic flows across the bridge might look like in the absence of any norm. Suppose a first driver arrives from the north, finds the bridge empty, and begins to cross. A split second later, a second driver arrives from the south and, seeing a car already on the bridge coming from the opposite direction, decides to wait for the first driver to finish crossing. After all, it would be foolish to enter the bridge before then, since that would necessitate one of the drivers having to back off the bridge before either could cross.

First-come, first-served: Not always an efficient norm.

But with the first driver only ten seconds into his thirty-second crossing, suppose a third driver arrives, also from the north, and enters the bridge. Again, the second driver's best bet is to continue waiting. If additional cars arrived from the north at intervals of less than thirty seconds, each could enter the bridge in the wake of the preceding car, further prolonging the second driver's wait. In periods of relatively heavy traffic, drivers arriving from the south might thus have to wait for hours before crossing.

Ithaca's social norm attempts to eliminate that possibility by calling for drivers to cross the bridge in the order in which they arrive from either direction. In the situation described above, the norm exhorts the third driver not to enter the bridge until the second driver has finished crossing. This requires restraint, because if the third driver had begun crossing the bridge in the wake of the first car, the second driver could do nothing about it. He would have to wait until the third driver (and others close on his heels) had finished crossing.

How well does this norm work? When traffic is heavy from both directions, waiting times are actually longer than if the norm did not exist.

Suppose a ten-car caravan arrived from each direction, with ten seconds separating the cars in each caravan, and with the first driver in the northbound caravan reaching the bridge a split second before his counterpart in the southbound caravan. If no one followed the first-come, first-served norm, all northbound cars would cross the bridge, after which the ten southbound cars would cross. Northbound cars would experience no wait at all, and as readers with a pencil, paper, and a little patience can easily verify, the southbound drivers would experience total combined waiting time of twelve minutes and thirty seconds.

In contrast, if all followed the first-come, first-served norm, the first northbound car would cross, followed by the first southbound car, then the second northbound car, followed by the second southbound car, and so on. If you are patient enough to add up the relevant waiting times, you will see that total waiting time would be 80 minutes—37.5 minutes for northbound cars and 42.5 minutes for southbound cars—more than six times as long as when there was no norm.

The first-come, first-served norm not only increases total waiting time substantially but also makes the distribution of waiting times more uneven. But these problems are significant only during periods of heavy traffic flow, which in Ithaca are relatively rare.

Despite its flaws, the first-come, first-served norm has proved durable. After each crossing, it is common for drivers to salute the driver at the head of the queue on the opposite side, acknowledging that he could have sped onto the bridge in the wake of the car ahead of him yet did not.

10

The Informal Market for Personal Relationships

Although social relationships are influenced largely by sentiment, they are by no means exempt from economic logic. Consider, for example, the link between wealth and personal attractiveness. Everyone wants a home in a safe neighborhood with good schools, but those with low incomes cannot be sure of getting one. So economists are not surprised that women mention earning power at or near the top of the list when surveyed about traits they find attractive in men.

In F. Scott Fitzgerald's novel *The Great Gatsby*, James Gatz understands that his humble station in life makes him an unlikely suitor for the hand of his coveted Daisy. So he renames himself Jay Gatsby and labors with singular focus and determination to achieve material success on the grandest scale possible.

Adam Smith's theory of compensating wage differentials (see Chapter 3) helps illuminate a particular detail of Gatsby's quest. This theory holds that the more unpleasant and risky a job is, the more it pays. Some of the largest pay premiums, it turns out, go to highly qualified people who are willing to do morally questionable work. Gatsby realized that to have any chance of achieving his goal, he could not be cautious or squeamish.

Fitzgerald never reveals the precise details of how Gatsby amassed his fortune. But he leaves little doubt that Gatsby's work was not just morally suspect but well outside the law. Gatsby surely realized that if he were caught and punished, his dream would evaporate. But a less risky path would have meant certain failure.

The examples in this chapter exploit the economist's view that the informal market for social relationships is subject to the same logic of supply and demand that governs behavior in other markets. In advancing this claim, economists do not insist that love plays no role in the choice of a marriage partner. Indeed, Fitzgerald himself, who clearly embraced the view that material concerns are important in the search for a mate, is said to have advised friends not to marry for money. "Go where the money is," he counseled, "then marry for love."

Although each of the 6 billion people on the planet differs from all others in any number of ways, there are certain common characteristics that people seem to value in potential marriage partners. These differ from culture to culture, but there is a surprising degree of overlap. Large numbers of people, for example, prefer partners who are kind, honest, loyal, healthy, intelligent, and physically attractive. Women generally confess to being attracted to men who are financially successful. Although men never used to mention earning power when asked to list what they find attractive in a woman, they have begun to do so in recent U.S. surveys.

The purchasing power that each person brings to the informal market for marriage partners is his or her endowment of personal characteristics. To simplify discussion, it is common to measure a searcher's purchasing power as a weighted average of the personal characteristics he or she possesses, where the individual weights represent the relative importance of the corresponding characteristics. Each person might thus be assigned an index number from 1 to 10, with higher numbers representing more desirable combinations of personal characteristics. Each searcher is then assumed to follow the rule "Marry the best person who will have you," and the result is an assortative mating pattern in which the 10s pair with other 10s, the 9s with other 9s, and so on.

Needless to say, this is a crassly unsentimental description of how people sort themselves into couples. Yet it seems to provide at least rough insights into some of the courtship behaviors we actually observe.

Why has the average age at first marriage increased? *(Justin Grimm)*

In the United States, the average age at first marriage in 1960 was 22.8 years for men and 20.3 years for women. By 2004 these ages had increased to 27.4 and 25.8 respectively. Similar increases have taken place in other countries. The average age at first marriage in Australia in 2001 was 28.7 for men and 26.9 for women, up from 23.4 for men and 21.1 for women in 1970. Why are people waiting longer to get married?

One reason is that as rising incomes have produced greater access to higher education, the amount of education a person needs to land any given job has increased. For example, whereas a person with a high school diploma might have reasonably expected to get a job as a bank teller a century ago, most banks today fill such positions with college graduates. And as labor markets have become more competitive, grades and other measures of school performance have had an increasing impact on career success.

On both accounts, the opportunity cost of marrying young has been increasing. For instance, early marriage makes it more difficult to pursue a college diploma, especially for parents. And to the extent that people hope to marry someone prosperous, the information required to predict success is not available as soon as it used to be.

Traditionally, one of the perceived benefits of marrying young was to pair up with an attractive partner before all the good ones were claimed. But there may be fewer reasons than in the past to worry about being left behind. With higher income, education, and mobility has come access to a steadily growing pool of potential marriage partners. So the opportunity cost of passing on an attractive partner when young is not as high as it once was.

Another perceived benefit of marrying young was to have children while one was still healthy and strong enough to meet the demands of raising them. But this benefit has also diminished with improvements in health and longevity.

In short, the costs of marrying young have been rising, while the benefits have been declining. And that may help explain why the average age at first marriage has been rising.

Why is it easier to find a partner when you already have one? *(Hetal Petal)*

A young man became close friends with an attractive young woman. Their relationship was strictly platonic. One evening, the woman invited her friend to a bar, saying, "I'm going to help you meet someone tonight." The two went to the bar, where the woman was uncharacteristically attentive. As they sat there, in full view of other patrons, she caressed his arm, gazed lovingly into his eyes, and whispered frequently in his ear. Then she announced her departure, asking him to meet her for coffee the next day. After she left the bar, several other attractive young women made contact with the young man. This took him completely by surprise. Why were these women suddenly showing such interest in him?

Over coffee the next day, his friend was unsurprised by his account of all the attention he'd received, saying, "I knew perfectly well what would happen."

"It's hard to tell whether someone's okay just by looking at him," she explained. But because other women in the bar understood that attractive women are generally much in demand by men, the fact that she, an attractive woman, was paying such close attention to a man she obviously knew well was a credible signal that he was okay.

The young man saw this experience as yet another example of the Matthew effect: "For unto every one that hath shall be given, and he shall have abundance" (Matthew 25:29). Or, when it rains it pours!

Why is coyness often considered an attractive attribute?

Single men and women of marriageable age often go to considerable lengths to meet potential spouses. They frequent bars, join clubs, purchase gym memberships, attend religious services, enlist the help of friends and relatives, and patronize dating services. Yet they often reject seemingly attractive potential mates who seem overly eager to form relationships. Why this preference for coyness in potential partners?

The late Groucho Marx once said that he wouldn't want to belong to any club that would have him as a member. It would of course be a clear recipe for failure to take this posture in the search for a personal relationship. Yet Marx was clearly on to something.

As noted, people commonly seek partners who are compassionate, intelligent, healthy, honest, emotionally stable, and physically attractive. Some of these characteristics are easy to observe, others less so. Someone who had all of these qualities would be in great demand and thus unlikely to be desperate for a partner. But the same would not be true of people who knew themselves to be deficient in many of the traits that are most difficult to observe. These people are more likely to have experienced repeated rejections and may find it difficult to conceal their eagerness to achieve success.

The upshot is that coyness, within limits, is an attractive attribute. People who know themselves to be attractive are seldom desperate to land a partner.

Why do people living in rural areas marry younger than those in urban areas?
(Matt Hagen)

Between 2000 and 2003 the average age at first marriage in largely rural West Virginia was 25.9 years for men and 23.9 years for women. In contrast, the average age at first marriage in largely urban/suburban New Jersey was 28.6 for men and 26.4 for women. Why are people who live in rural areas quicker to marry?

One cost of marrying young is a greater likelihood of divorce. All couples, urban and rural, would thus be more likely to enjoy enduring marriages if they waited a little longer before tying the knot. But as we have seen, choices that make sense for the population as a whole are not always attractive to individuals. When someone meets an especially attractive marriage partner, for example, he or she might see not only the advantages of waiting longer but also the risks—in particular, the possibility that someone else might snap up that special person.

Although no two people are alike, if someone misses an opportunity to marry an attractive potential spouse in a large city, there remains a sufficiently large pool of single young people that a reasonably close substitute is likely to turn up eventually. But myriad idiosyncratic characteristics form the basis of human attraction, and when the opportunity for a promising relationship is missed in a rural setting, there is every reason to worry that the next-best option won't be nearly as attractive.

Early marriage in rural areas may thus be another example of the familiar conflict between individual and group incentives. Although it would be better for all to wait, the dominant strategy for each individual may be to snap up the first strong opportunity that comes along.

Another relevant difference is that educational levels tend to be lower in rural areas, and there are proportionately fewer people in high-achievement careers that take time to establish. So one incentive for waiting to marry—that the information required to predict success becomes available relatively late—doesn't apply as strongly in rural areas.

THE ECONOMIST'S MODEL of the market for relationships sheds light on not only courtship practices but also the laws by which societies regulate marriage and the decisions people make about whether to stay married.

If polygamy benefits men and harms women, as is commonly assumed, why do predominantly male legislatures prohibit it?

Many people believe that consenting adults should be free to do as they please, provided they do not cause unacceptable harm to others. The difficult question, of course, is what constitutes unacceptable harm. *Big Love,* the HBO television series about a fictional polygamous family in Salt Lake City, has touched off renewed debate about this question.

Barb, Nicki, and Margene, the three heroines of *Big Love,* chose to marry Bill Henrickson, a successful businessman able to provide generously for their extended family. Should society outlaw such arrangements because they cause unacceptable harm to others? If so, who is harmed, exactly, and how? The economist's model of the informal market for marriage partners, it turns out, has interesting things to say about these questions.

The traditional argument against plural marriage is that it harms women, particularly young girls who may be coerced into such marriages. Needless to say, society should prohibit forced participation in any marriage, plural or monogamous. But mature women who freely choose plural marriage reveal a preference for that arrangement. So if plural marriage harms women, the victims must be those who prefer monogamy.

It is easy to see how some of these women may be harmed. In a monogamous world, for example, Barb's first choice might have been to marry Bill, who would also have chosen to marry her. But with plural marriage permissible, Bill might prefer to marry not just Barb but also Nicki and Margene. Barb would then have to choose between two lesser outcomes: a continued search for a monogamous partner or a plural marriage not to her liking.

The mere fact that allowing plural marriage may eliminate attractive options for some women does not imply that it imposes unacceptable harm on women generally. Suppose, for example, that if polygamy were legal, 10 percent of adult men would take an average of three wives apiece and all remaining marriages would be monogamous. Among aspiring monogamists, there would then be nine men for every seven women. With an excess of men in the informal market for monogamous partners, the terms of exchange would shift in favor of women. Wives would change fewer diapers, and their parents might even escape paying for weddings.

What about men? Here, too, plural marriage would clearly benefit some. After all, there are surely other men like Bill Henrickson of *Big Love* who would not only prefer multiple wives but also attract them.

But what about those who prefer monogamy? Permitting plural unions would, as noted, create an imbalance of men over women among monogamists. With so many formerly eligible women no longer available, the terms of exchange would turn sharply against men (as has happened in China as a result of female infanticide). Many men could not marry at all.

In short, the logic of supply and demand turns the conventional wisdom about plural marriage on its head. If the arrangement harms anyone, the more likely victims are men, not women.

This conclusion is reinforced if we take account of the costly, and mutually offsetting, jockeying for position associated with men's attempts to win the attention of scarce women. With women in chronically short supply, men would face even more intense pressure than they do now to get ahead economically and spend even longer hours honing their abs. More men would undergo cosmetic surgery. Expenditures on engagement rings would rise. Valentine's Day bouquets would be *two* dozen roses. Yet no matter how valiantly each man strove, the same number would be destined not to marry.

Whatever other purposes they may serve, laws against plural marriage function as positional arms control agreements that make life less stressful for men. This may help explain their appeal to predominantly male legislatures.

Why might so many military marriages dissolve after ten years?
(Andrew Blanco)

According to one early study, the probability that a given couple will divorce peaks in the third year of marriage, drops sharply through the seventh year, and declines more gradually thereafter. But according to military folklore, couples in which one partner is a member of the armed services experience a significant upturn in divorce rates during the eleventh year of marriage. What might explain this difference?

A plausible hyphothesis is suggested by the terms of the Uniformed Services Former Spouses Protection Act (USFSPA), which establishes the terms under which divorced spouses may exercise claims against their former military spouse's military retirement benefits. After ten years of marriage concurrent with military service, the former spouse is entitled under USFSPA to a pro-rated share of his or her former partner's military retirement pension via direct payment from the Defense Finance and Accounting Service. By waiting to divorce after the tenth anniversary, former military spouses thus avoid having to rely on their ex-spouses to make good on pension shares awarded in divorce settlements.

THE INFORMAL MARKET for marriage partners may even influence the patterns of traits we observe in people, as well as how specific traits and preferences are likely to affect people's choices.

Why are physically attractive people also more intelligent than others, on average? *(Satoshi Kanazawa, Jody Kovar)*

Research has shown that people who are regarded as physically attractive also tend to be seen as more intelligent. And it has often been noted that attractive children tend to receive higher grades in school. Although the latter finding has often been interpreted as evidence of teacher bias, an economic analysis of the informal market for marriage partners suggests that better-looking children may actually be smarter.

Evolutionary psychologists Satoshi Kanazawa and Jody Kovar, for example, offer persuasive evidence for the following four propositions: (1) More intelligent men tend to achieve higher social status and higher incomes. (2) Men generally regard physically attractive women as more desirable marriage partners. (3) Women generally regard men with higher incomes and higher social status as more desirable marriage partners. (4) Both intelligence and physical attractiveness are traits with significant heritable components. If the first three propositions are true, then it follows logically that relatively attractive women will pair up disproportionately with relatively intelligent men. And if both beauty and intelligence are heritable, then the offspring of such unions will tend to display above-average values of both traits.

In short, given what we know about the informal market for personal relationships, the hypothesis that beauty and brains go together does not appear far-fetched.

Why might a man who prefers brunettes be likely to marry a kinder, healthier, prettier, more intelligent woman than a man with a preference for blondes?

It is said that gentlemen prefer blondes, and in many Western countries survey evidence confirms this. But suppose a man could choose which hair color he found most attractive. Might he have good reasons to prefer brunettes?

Again, each man's purchasing power in the informal market for marriage partners is the index value assigned by the market to his particular mix of personal characteristics. For any given man, that index is fixed, at least in the short run. The model's basic claim is that men with a given index value end up pairing with women with similar index values. Thus a 9-point man might hope to marry a 10-point woman, but that woman would generally have better options. Realistically, a 9-point man can expect to marry a 9-point woman.

But for people of either sex, a wide variety of combinations of personal characteristics could produce an index value of 9. Among such people, higher values for any individual characteristic imply lower values for all other characteristics. Thus, if being blonde contributes positively to a woman's attractiveness index, then a 9-point blonde will tend to have less favorable values than a 9-point brunette for all other characteristics that enter the mix. On the average, she will be less healthy, less intelligent, less kind, and less pretty on dimensions other than hair color. So if a gentleman could choose to prefer brunettes, he might have good reasons for doing so.

If attractive people are more intelligent than others, and if blondes are considered more attractive, why are there so many jokes about dumb blondes?

A quick web search identifies thousands of jokes about dumb blondes, such as: A married couple was asleep when the telephone rang at two in the morning. The wife, a blonde, picked up the telephone, listened a moment and said, "How should I know, that's two hundred miles from here!" and hung up. The husband said, "Who was that?" The wife said, "I don't know; some woman wanting to know if the coast is clear."

These jokes pose an economic puzzle. As noted, evidence suggests that men find blondes more attractive than brunettes. There is also evidence suggesting that people regarded as attractive tend to be more intelligent than average. Why, then, are there so many jokes about dumb blondes?

How intelligent other people think you are depends not only on your native mental abilities, but also on the extent to which you cultivate them through investment in education and training. In turn, the

© Scott Adams, Inc. / Dist. by UFS, Inc.

amount a person chooses to invest in education depends on how the return on such investments compares with those on alternative investments. If blondes are indeed perceived as being more attractive, then
being blonde may create attractive opportunities that do not require
heavy investments in education.

The perception that blondes are less intelligent than others may thus
stem less from any innate difference in their mental abilities than from
the fact that they rationally choose to invest less in education. Or perhaps jealous brunettes with time on their hands find it satisfying to sit
around making up dumb blonde jokes.

CRITICS RIGHTLY OBJECT that the economist's flinty-eyed model of
the implicit market for personal relationships misses much that is important. Although the model helps explain certain patterns of
courtship, it ignores the critical element of commitment in successful
marriages, which by its nature must be largely independent of material considerations.

The importance of commitment in bilateral relationships is familiar
to anyone who has ever dealt with a landlord. Suppose, for example, you
have just moved to a new city and need to find an apartment. If you are
in Los Angeles or some other metropolis, you cannot possibly inspect
each of the thousands of vacant apartments, so you check the listings
and visit a few to get a rough idea of what is available—the range of
prices, amenities, locations, and other features you care about. As your
search proceeds, you find a unit that seems unusually attractive on the
basis of your impressions of the relevant distributions. You want to close
the deal. At that point, you *know* there is a better apartment out there

somewhere, but your time is too valuable to justify looking further. You want to get on with your life.

Having made that decision, the next important step is to make a commitment with the owner of the apartment. You do not want to move in and then be told to leave a month later. By then you will have bought curtains, hung your art on the walls, installed phone and cable service, and so on. If you are forced to leave, not only will those investments be for naught, you will also have to begin searching anew for a place to live.

The landlord also has an interest in your staying for an extended period, since he went to a lot of trouble and expense to rent the apartment. He advertised it and showed it to dozens of prospective tenants, none of whom seemed quite as stable and trustworthy as you.

The upshot is that even though you know there is a better apartment out there, and even though your landlord knows there is a better tenant, you both have a strong interest in committing yourselves to ignore such opportunities. The standard solution is to sign a lease—a contract that prevents each of you from accepting other offers that might later prove attractive. If you move out, you must still pay your rent for the duration of the lease. If your landlord asks you to leave, the lease empowers you to refuse.

The ability to commit by signing a lease raises the amount a tenant would be willing to pay for any given apartment and reduces the amount its owner would be willing to accept. Without the security provided by this contractual commitment, many valuable exchanges would never occur. Leases foreclose valuable options, but that is exactly what the signers want them to do.

In searching for a mate, you confront an essentially similar commitment problem. You want a mate but not just anyone. After dating for a while, you feel you know a fair amount about what kinds of people are out there—what sorts of dispositions they have, their ethical values, their cultural and recreational interests, their social and professional skills, and so on. Among those you meet, you are drawn to one in particular. Your luck holds, and that person feels the same way about you. You both want to move forward and start investing in your relationship. You want to get married, buy a house, have children. Few of these steps make sense, however, unless you both expect your relationship to continue for an extended period.

But what if something goes wrong? No matter what your mate's vision of the ideal partner may be, you know there's someone out there who comes closer to that ideal than you. What if that person suddenly shows up? Or one of you falls ill? Just as landlords and tenants can gain by committing themselves, partners in marriage have a similar interest in foreclosing future options.

The marriage contract is one way of attempting to achieve the desired commitment. On reflection, however, we see that a legal contract is not particularly well suited to creating the kind of commitment both parties want. Even fiercely draconian legal sanctions can only force people to remain with spouses they would prefer to leave. But marriage on those terms hardly serves the goals each partner had originally hoped to achieve.

A far more secure commitment results if the legal contract is reinforced by bonds of affection. The plain fact is that many relationships are not threatened when a new potential partner who is kinder, wealthier, more charming, and better looking comes along. Someone who has become emotionally attached to his or her spouse does not *want* to pursue new opportunities, even ones that, in purely objective terms, might seem more promising.

That is not to say that emotional commitments are fail-safe. Who among us would not experience at least mild concern upon hearing that his wife was having dinner with George Clooney this evening, or that her husband was having a drink with Scarlett Johansson? Yet even imperfect emotional commitments free most couples from such concerns most of the time.

The important point is that even though such emotional commitments foreclose potentially valuable opportunities, they also confer important benefits. An emotional commitment to one's spouse is valuable in the coldly rational cost-benefit calculus because it promotes fitness-enhancing investments. But note the ironic twist. These commitments work best when they deflect people from thinking explicitly about their spousal relationships in cost-benefit terms.

Evidence suggests that people who consciously approach those relationships in scorekeeping terms are less satisfied with their marriages than others; and when therapists try to get people to think in cost-benefit terms about their relationships, it often seems to backfire. That may not be the way evolution designed us to think about personal relationships.

11
Two Originals

One of the difficult decisions I faced when I began writing this book was the extent to which I would modify the student essays on which a majority of the examples are based. Although many essays posed interesting questions, sometimes the answers were not clearly explained or didn't quite make economic sense. If these questions were to be included, I had little choice but to modify the corresponding explanations.

Yet many other essays posed interesting questions in which the explanations were not only crystal clear but written in wonderfully spirited language. It was those essays I agonized most about before finally concluding that the book would be an easier read if written in a single voice throughout. So I rewrote from scratch all the answers to the questions posed by my students. In at least some instances, I am sorry to report, my reconstructions don't really do justice to the originals. To those authors, I sincerely apologize.

To illustrate how delightful many of the original essays were, I've reproduced two of them here almost word for word:

Why do animal rights activists target fur-wearing women but leave leather-clad bikers alone? *(Kevin Heisey)*

There are several possible logical explanations, three of which I'll examine here. The first, and probably the most obvious, looks at the physical, evolutionary advantages of harassing older women versus burly bikers. The second considers the total number of animals it takes to make a fur coat versus a leather jacket, and the final possible explanation examines the activist's behavior from a cost-benefit analysis view, where the benefit is gaining converts to their cause at a cost of alienating some people.

When this question is considered from an evolutionary perspective, the advantages to activists targeting fur wearers are clear. There is little physical risk involved in splattering red paint on a woman's fur coat. Maybe you'll get a blow from a swinging purse, but a young, agile animal rights activist should be able to avoid even this threat. On the other hand, picture the same activist splattering red paint on a biker's leather jacket. The activist, if lucky, would be facing a chase and more likely than not kicking and punching, and possibly weapons from the victim and his or her friends. It is easy to see how the activists with an inclination to protest fur would have an evolutionary advantage over those protesting leather in this environment. So can we conclude that animal rights activists carry or have developed the traits of cowardly bullies? There is a certain logic behind the conclusion, but I think it is too simplistic.

Perhaps animal activists feel, in a finite world with limited time and resources, they should strategically target the activities that abuse the most animals. Following this thinking, several mink, ermine, or foxes are needed to produce a fur coat, while a leather jacket can probably be produced with one cow. By targeting the fur wearer, the activist is standing up for and protesting the deaths of several animals. The leather-wearer is only carrying around one dead animal. So maybe the activists feel it is a more efficient use of scarce resources to target fur. There is a flaw in this logic, however. Sure, individually a fur wearer is responsible for the deaths of more animals, but in society as a whole many more cattle are killed for the use of people than minks or foxes. By the logic of using limited resources efficiently to protest the deaths of animals, the activists should be more likely to target leather wearers since they are more prevalent in society.

Finally, let me make some different assumptions about activists' motives. Suppose their motive is to convert more sympathizers to their cause. Also, suppose the cost of converting sympathizers is the number of people alienated by the activism. The objective is to convert as many people as possible at the lowest cost. First, let's look at the targeting of fur wearers. Fur wearers are typically wealthy older women; wearing fur is often viewed as conspicuous consumption; and the creatures used for fur are cute and generate sympathy. Targeting fur wearers doesn't alienate a great number of people. Generally the victims of the protest don't generate a lot of sympathy whereas the animal victims do.

Compare that with the leather-clad biker. On the surface, the bikers don't generate a lot of sympathy either. Sure, if targeted by animal rights activists they may generate support in a twisted "lions versus Christians" way. I can see it in the video stores now, right next to "Coleslaw Wrestling at Sturgis, Vol. IV," you could have "Bikers Stomp PETA, Vol. II." Looking beyond that, though, what is it that bikers do on, say, Independence Day? They ride in formation with their biker friends to a gathering place where they grill steaks and hamburgers, drink beer, and shoot fireworks when the sun goes down. Take away the riding in formation, and it is pretty much the same thing everyone else does on Independence Day. So targeting bikers for wearing leather could easily gain fewer sympathizers to the activists' cause and has the potential to alienate far more people. Not many people have a fur coat in their wardrobe, but most have leather shoes or a belt, if not a leather jacket. Also, most eat beef. So it's plausible that the rationale behind animal rights activists targeting fur wearers has little to do with cowardice or physical survival. It could be that it is the most efficient net generator of supporters to their cause.

Crouching Talent, Hidden Costs: Will special effects drive the world's most talented choreographer from the market? *(Jacob Lehman)*

Until 1999, Yuen Wo-Ping was an unknown fight choreographer, even among the knowledgeable, in the United States. Since his flying fights in *The Matrix* and *Crouching Tiger, Hidden Dragon,* there is an almost limitless demand for his services. Meanwhile, William Hobbs, arguably the greatest choreographer in the world, having worked on *Rob Roy*, *Dangerous Liaisons*, *The Count of Monte Christo*, and *The Three Musketeers* (1974), among others, retains his modest appeal. Hobbs's fights are renowned among choreographers and enthusiasts for their historical accuracy, as he refuses to incorporate moves that are not found in combat manuals from the time periods in question. Wo-Ping, on the other hand, makes extensive use of super-high-speed wire-fu, which only minimally reflects actual combat techniques.

Wo-Ping's flashy fights, which resemble video games as much as combat, are controversial. They contain little narrative value compared to Hobbs's realistic, emotionally charged conflicts, but they make for excellent clips in previews and advertisements. As a result, Wo-Ping has captured household recognition remarkably well, thereby giving him an advantage in the winner-take-all market of fight choreography. The costs of his fantasy fights are significant. First, they decrease popular appreciation for the skill incorporated in Hobbs's work, and second, they drive others to speed up their fights, use more wires, and reach out further on that spectrum just to get an audience. Even Jackie Chan, long the champion of realism in stunts, has resorted to wire work in his recent movies, rather than continuing to perform his own nearly impossible but very real stunts. There is an inspirational and educational value to seeing what humans are truly capable of in terms of speed, storytelling, and stunts. The push toward digital effects and harness work undermines our natural astonishment at the gifts of the truly talented, and only serves to further the gap between reality and what we see on screen. The rewards to the winners in such a winner-take-all market, however, are great enough that the costs of taking an additional step from reality seem small to the individual compared to the profits from that advantage. Society, however, gains no additional benefit from films in which people take thirty steps up a wall compared to those in which people take only three. It is not in Wo-Ping's (or any other entrant's) interest to consider this cost, nor the loss of popularity of William Hobbs and Jackie Chan as a result of his entry. This will result in "too many contestants" in the winner-take-all market, with not only zero profit for society, but even a net cost as effects grow more important compared to training and talent.

Parting Thoughts

Just by having read this far, you are well on the road to becoming an economic naturalist. You may have already described some of the book's examples to family members and friends. If so, each of these conversations will have deepened your understanding of the economic principles they illustrate.

In the kingdom of the blind, the one-eyed man is king. As I noted in the Introduction, even those who have taken an economics course in college typically emerge with little working knowledge of basic economic principles. In relative terms, therefore, you are already an economics expert.

Perhaps you have also begun to recognize new details and patterns in the things you observe each day. In all likelihood, you've already encountered numerous examples of discount hurdles as you shop. If it's a stiff challenge you want, try to find examples of products that are never made available at discount prices to buyers who are willing to clear some sort of hurdle. There are such products, but they are rare. Trying to spot them will call your attention to a variety of interesting hurdles you'd never noticed before.

If a friend asked you why so many stores put sheets and towels on sale in January each year, you could probably cobble together a plausible economic explanation. By offering discounts, you'd explain, sellers can sell additional units to people who wouldn't have bought without them. The seller's challenge, of course, is to prevent buyers who are willing to pay full list price from buying at deep discounts. You'd describe to your friend how the January white sales confront buyers with two specific hurdles that serve this purpose. First, the aspiring discount shopper must take the trouble to inform herself when the goods will be put on sale; and second, she must summon the patience to postpone her purchases until then. These hurdles work, you'd explain, because the people willing to jump them usually would not have bought linens at all in a given year, or at least not as many, if not for the deep discounts.

Your friend might ask why others don't jump the hurdles as well. People whose opportunity cost of time is high, you'd respond, generally find them too bothersome to jump. If Bill and Melinda Gates want some extra towels in June, they don't wait until January to buy them. Such people typically end up paying the full list price.

If someone asked you why manufacturers offer discounts to buyers who mail in rebate coupons, you'd offer a similar explanation. People whose opportunity cost of time is low are often those who wouldn't, or couldn't, buy the product except at a discount. It is these people who are disproportionately willing to take the time to mail in coupons and wait patiently for their rebate checks to arrive as much as six months later. My mother, the quintessential price-sensitive shopper, does this all the time. If you do it, then you, too, are almost certainly a highly price-sensitive shopper. But if you have never taken the trouble to mail in a rebate coupon, then you almost certainly are not. Sellers don't want to give you a discount because they know you're just as likely to buy their products without one.

Having seen many examples of ways in which the interests of individuals and groups fail to coincide, you'll be quick to notice many others. If you have children in high school, for instance, you may be more likely to notice that although taking SAT prep courses now seems almost essential for students aspiring to enter top universities, the vast amounts of time and money spent on these courses serve little purpose for students as a group. The quest for admission to a top university is essentially a contest, and no matter how valiantly people strive in any contest, the number of prizes remains limited.

It's surprising how many such contests there are, and how hard it is to find one whose contestants do not engage in behaviors that are functionally equivalent to a wasteful military arms race. In college football, for example, schools try to enhance their odds of winning by spending more on coaches, recruiting, training facilities, and the like. Yet no matter how much schools spend, no more than half the teams that play on any given Saturday can win.

The wastefulness of mutually offsetting investments in performance enhancement has not escaped notice. In virtually all cases, governing bodies have implemented a variety of measures to limit such investments. For example, engine displacement in Formula 1 racing cars is limited to 2.4 liters, sparing contestants from having to invest in larger engines. Similarly, all professional sports leagues impose strict limits on team rosters, thus limiting the cost of fielding competitive teams.

Agreements to limit arms races are by no means confined to formal athletic competition. Rewards in many important domains of life depend strongly on relative performance. Thus, as we saw in earlier chapters, mandatory kindergarten start dates, school uniform requirements, workplace safety regulations, and even laws that prohibit polygamy all serve to curb arms races of various sorts. If you like stiff challenges, here's another: try to find an example of an organized activity that rewards relative performance but has made no attempt to limit contestants' mutually offsetting investments in performance enhancement. If such an activity exists, I have not yet encountered it. Rules are data. Observe the rules that various groups impose and try to figure out what their purpose might be.

If you are thinking about changing jobs or have children who are considering what careers to pursue, the examples illustrating the theory of compensating wage differentials may have special relevance. Or so I am inclined to believe, having noticed how this theory has often led my students to think more intelligently about their career choices. Many of them begin with the single, overriding goal of finding the highest possible salary. But as we have seen, any given person's highest-paying offer will inevitably entail concessions on other important dimensions of job satisfaction. Because jobs that entail moral compromise, inflexible work schedules, poor promotion prospects, and low employment security are generally viewed as less attractive, they must pay more to compensate for those attributes.

Some people would willingly accept these trade-offs in exchange for higher pay, but others are unaware the trade-offs exist. Even in your early days as an economic naturalist, you are well positioned to realize that the highest-paying offer demands special scrutiny. If it seems to be too good to be true, it probably is.

You are also well positioned to know when information can be taken at face value and when it invites skepticism. If the interests of two parties coincide perfectly, they have no incentive to mislead each other. Thus when a bridge player employs standard bidding conventions to signal the strength of her hand to her partner, her statement need only be intelligible. Her partner has no reason to question its sincerity. But when a seller touts the quality of his product, the buyer has ample reason to be wary. The economic naturalist knows that such statements are credible only if they are costly to fake. The offer of a comprehensive guarantee, for example, is a relatively reliable signal of product quality, since the seller of a low-quality product could not profitably extend such an offer.

The no cash on the table principle warns an economic naturalist to take the prognostications of investment advisers with a grain of salt. If an adviser claims a company's stock is underpriced, he or she is saying in effect that there is cash on the table. Yet cash on the table seldom sits unclaimed for long. If others knew the stock was underpriced, the economic naturalist knows to wonder why didn't they rush to buy it, thus driving up its price. Is the adviser claiming to have inside information? Savvy economic naturalists recognize those who promise overnight riches from buying underpriced stocks as the charlatans they are.

But beyond how your skills as an economic naturalist may help you make better decisions in the marketplace, there are ample rewards in continuing to develop them. Virtually every feature of the built environment, virtually every feature of human and animal behavior, is the explicit or implicit result of the interplay of costs and benefits. There are rich textures and patterns in everyday experience that become visible to the practiced eye of the economic naturalist. Discovering them is an intellectual adventure you can savor for the rest of your days.

Notes

Introduction

3   *Nineteen percent of American undergraduates take only one economics course:*
W. L. Hansen, M. K. Salemi, and J. J. Siegfried, "Use It or Lose It: Teaching Economic Literacy," *American Economic Review* (Papers and Proceedings), May 2002, 463–472.

3   *when students are given tests designed to probe their knowledge of basic economics:* W. L. Hansen, M. K. Salemi, and J. J. Siegfried, "Use It or Lose It: Teaching Economic Literacy," *American Economic Review (Papers and Proceedings),* May 2002, 463–472.

4   *Yet we now have persuasive evidence that most students do not master this concept:* Paul J. Ferraro and Laura O. Taylor, "Do Economists Recognize an Opportunity Cost When They See One? A Dismal Performance from the Dismal Science," *B.E. Journals in Economic Analysis and Policy* 4, no. 1 (2005).

6   *For example, here is a standard Darwinian question:* For an excellent introduction to the Darwinian framework, see Richard Dawkins, *The Selfish Gene,* 3rd ed. (New York: Oxford University Press, 2006).

7   *The winners of these battles command nearly exclusive sexual access*: See www.pbs.org/wgbh/nova/bowerbirds/courtship.html.

9   *As Walter Doyle and Kathy Carter, two proponents of the narrative theory of learning, have written:* Walter Doyle and Kathy Carter, "Narrative and Learning to Teach: Implications for Teacher Education Curriculum," http://faculty.ed.uiuc.edu/westbury/JCS/Vol35/DOYLE.HTM.

9   *Psychologist Jerome Bruner:* Jerome Bruner, "Narrative and Paradigmatic Modes of Thought," in E. W. Eisner, ed., *Learning and Teaching the Ways of Knowing*, 84th Yearbook, pt. 2 of the National Society for the Study of Education (Chicago: University of Chicago Press, 1985), 97–115.

10   *Still, it is not always easy to apply:* The examples that follow are based on the work of psychologists Daniel Kahneman and the late Amos Tversky, citations to whose work appear repeatedly in the notes for Chapter 10.

12   *When Ben Bernanke and I described Bill Tjoa's example:* Robert H. Frank and Ben S. Bernanke, *Principles of Economics* (New York: McGraw-Hill, 2000).

12   *Sure enough, there is a requirement:* Section 4.34.4 of the *ADA Accessibility Guidelines for Buildings and Facilities* (Appendix to part 1191, 36 CFR chapter 11, issued pursuant to the Americans with Disabilities Act of 1990) says, "Instructions and all information for use [of an automated teller machine] shall be made accessible to and independently usable by persons with vision impairments."

Chapter 1 • Rectangular Milk Cartons and Cylindrical Soda Cans: The Economics of Product Design

19   *Making these cans shorter and wider would require substantially less aluminum:* See problem 4, "The Math Page," www.themathpage.com/aCalc/applied.htm.

24   *Research has shown that bright yellow is the best color:* S. S. Solomon and J. G. King, "Influence of Color on Fire Vehicle Accidents," *Journal of Safety Research* 26 (1995): 41–48; and S. S. Solomon, "Lime-Yellow Color As Related to Reduction of Serious Fire Apparatus Accidents: The Case for Visibility in Emergency Vehicle Accident Avoidance," *Journal of the American Optometric Association* 61 (1990): 827–831.

Chapter 2 • Free Peanuts and Expensive Batteries: Supply and Demand in Action

30   *Thus dairy farmers who were quick to adopt bovine somatotropin:* M. A. Tarrazon-Herrera et al., "Effects of Bovine Somatotropin on Milk Yield and Composition in Advanced Lactation Fed Low- or High-Energy Diets," *Journal of Dairy Science* 83 (2000): 430–434.

32   *The economist's model of supply and demand:* For a more detailed description of the supply and demand model, see chapter 3 of R. H. Frank and Ben S. Bernanke, *Principles of Economics*, 3rd ed. (New York: McGraw-Hill, 2006).

36   *retirees to abandon their existing homes:* Deborah Kades, "The Thing About a Lot of New Houses Is They're Big: Even Retired Couples Want a Lot of Room to Rattle Around In and for Visiting Grandchildren," *Capital Times & Wisconsin State Journal*, June 24, 2001, A5; Kelly Greene, "Florida Frets It Doesn't Have Enough Elderly," *Wall Street Journal*, October 18, 2002, B1.

42   *As Chris Anderson describes in his book: The Long Tail* (New York: Hyperion, 2006).

44   *According to the Egg Nutrition Center in Washington, D.C., neither the taste of an egg nor its nutritional quality:* ENC, "Egg Production," www.enc-online.org/trivia.htm.

45   *The brown hens tend to be larger than white ones:* See "Basic Egg Facts," http://gk12calbio.berkeley.edu/lessons/eggfacts.pdf.

50   *The top-ranked school cannot charge more because it needs its most accomplished students:* For an extended discussion of this issue, see R. H. Frank and P. J. Cook, *The Winner-Take-All Society* (New York: Free Press, 1995), chap. 8.

Chapter 3 • Why Equally Talented Workers Often Earn Different Salaries and Other Mysteries of the World of Work

51   *Fashion model Heidi Klum earned $7.5 million in 2005:* Forbes.com, "The Celebrity 100," www.forbes.com/2006/06/12/06celebrities_money-power-celebrities-list_land.html.

54   *Although many factors are involved, one in particular stands out—the rapid acceleration of technological changes that increase the leverage of the most able individuals:* For a detailed discussion of this interpretation, see R. H. Frank and P. J. Cook, *The Winner-Take-All Society* (New York: Free Press, 1995).

55   *But studies suggest that salary gains at the top have occurred primarily because executive decisions have become much more important to the bottom line:* See, for example, Xavier Gabaix and Augustin Landier, "Why Has CEO Pay Increased So Much?" MIT Department of Economics Work-

ing Paper no. 06-13, May 8, 2006. Available at SSRN: http://ssrn.com/ab-stract=901826.

57   *In the light of widely available scientific evidence that nicotine is in fact highly addictive:* See U.S. Surgeon General, *The Health Consequences of Smoking: Nicotine Addiction* (Washington, D.C.: United States Government Printing Office, 1988).

58   *Altria, the parent company of the Philip Morris:* Forbes.com, "CEO Compensation," www.forbes.com/lists/2006/12/Company_1.html.

59   *The resulting pay pattern in each firm is the functional equivalent of a progressive income tax:* For an extended discussion of this point, see R. H. Frank, *Choosing the Right Pond: Human Behavior and the Quest for Status* (New York: Oxford University Press, 1985), chaps. 3–4.

62   *One explanation for the observed time profile of wages:* For a formal development of this explanation, see Edward Lazear, "Agency, Earnings Profiles, Productivity, and Hours Restrictions," *American Economic Review* 71 (1981): 606–620.

63   *One possibility is that offering premium wages creates a bond that helps ensure honest behavior:* For an extended discussion of this possibility, see George Akerlof, "Labor Markets as Partial Gift Exchange," *Quarterly Journal of Economics*, November 1982, 543–569.

64   *When Napster introduced the first Internet music file-sharing program in 1999, established stars:* Barry Willis, "Napster Reinstates Some Users, Attacks Offspring, Angers Madonna," *Stereophile*, June 2000.

65   *According to a recent survey, the reason is that many taxi drivers work only as long:* Colin Camerer, Linda Babcock, George Loewenstein, and Richard Thaler, "Labor Supply of New York City Cab Drivers: One Day at a Time," *Quarterly Journal of Economics* 112 (1997): 407–442.

68   *So utilities serve short bursts of demand with peakers:* For a clear summary of how electric utilities use different types of equipment to serve loads of different duration, see Public Service Commission of Wisconsin, "Electric Power Plants," http://psc.wi.gov/thelibrary/publications/electric/electric04.pdf.

69   *inevitably kindle increased salary demands from in-house attorneys:* For a more extended discussion, see R. H. Frank, *Choosing the Right Pond* (New York: Oxford University Press, 1985).

70   *In such cases, the fact that HMO physicians bear the cost of the test:* For an extended discussion of how incentives affect physician behavior, see Martin

Gaynor, James Rebitzer, and Lowell Taylor, "Physician Incentives in HMOs," *Journal of Political Economy,* August 2004, 915–931.

Chapter 4 • Why Some Buyers Pay More Than Others: The Economics of Discount Pricing

72 *the seller permits the buyer to purchase at a discount, but only if the buyer is first willing to jump a hurdle:* For an extended discussion of the hurdle method of price discrimination, see Robert H. Frank and Ben S. Bernanke, *Principles of Economics,* 3rd ed. (New York: McGraw-Hill, 2006), chap. 10.

75 *By making discounts available to price-sensitive buyers without cutting prices to others:* For an extended discussion of how hurdle pricing often promotes efficiency, see R. H. Frank, "When Are Price Differentials Discriminatory?" *Journal of Policy Analysis and Management,* Winter 1983, 238–255.

84 *The clandestine way Starbucks markets the Short:* For a more extended discussion of the Starbucks Short, see Tim Harford, "Solving the Mystery of the Elusive 'Short' Cappuccino," *Slate*, January 6, 2006, www.slate.com/id/2133754.

Chapter 5 • Arms Races and the Tragedy of the Commons

96 *And if fishermen set sail whenever the net value of what they expect to catch exceeds their opportunity cost of time and other expenses:* Garrett Hardin, "The Tragedy of the Commons," *Science* 162 (1968): 1243–1248.

96 *Overprescription of antibiotics is a tragedy of the commons, much like the overharvesting of fish:* For an extended discussion of the problem of antibiotic resistance, see the Center for Disease Control and Prevention website at www.cdc.gov/drugresistance/community.

97 *But Austen describes Elinor's sister Marianne: Sense and Sensibility* (Philadelphia: Courage, 1996), p. 44.

97 *Men like an exaggerated female figure:* Caroline Cox, *Stiletto* (New York: Collins Design, 2004).

103 *To judge from their behavior, the benefit seems to exceed the cost:* For a lively discussion of this example and a host of related ones, see Thomas

Schelling, *Micromotives and Macrobehavior* (New York: Norton, 1978). This book, abrim with stimulating ideas, is also a fabulous read.

104   *Hence the attraction of helmet rules:* Thomas Schelling, *Micromotives and Macrobehavior* (New York: Norton, 1978).

Chapter 6 • The Myth of Ownership

109   *But while property rights create enormous benefits:* For an extended discussion of this point, see Stephen Holmes and Cass Sunstein, *The Cost of Rights: Why Liberty Depends on Taxes* (New York: Norton, 1999).

110   *The Ploofs later filed suit against Putnam, and a Vermont court found in their favor:* See *Ploof v. Putnam, 81 Vt. 471, 71 A. 188* (1908).

112   *A parsimonious explanation for why the two groups of Native Americans followed such different approaches:* For a more detailed discussion of this issue, see Martin Bailey, "Approximate Optimality of Aboriginal Property Rights," *Journal of Law and Economics*, April 1992, 183–198.

113   *They have a simple economic rationale—the interests of the community are not well served by allowing valuable property to sit unused:* For an extended discussion of squatters rights, see Cora Jordan, "Trespass, Adverse Possession, and Easements," Lectric Law Library, www.lectlaw.com/files/lat06.htm.

115   *The rarest and most precious variety comes from the Beluga sturgeon, which can grow up to 30 feet long:* For a detailed description of this remarkable fish, see Prosanta Chakrabarty, "Huso Huso (Beluga Sturgeon)," Animal Diversity Web, University of Michigan Museum of Zoology, http://animal-diversity.ummz.umich.edu/site/accounts/information/Huso_huso.html.

117   *For the most part, we either buy books from commercial bookstores or borrow them without charge from public libraries:* In 2004 Blockbuster Video launched Bookbuster, a book rental venture. With weekly rental rates of $5.99 for recently published books, this service has attracted relatively few customers.

120   *workers who are free to sell their safety for higher wages may realize:* For a more detailed discussion of this rationale for safety regulation, see R. H. Frank, *Choosing the Right Pond* (New York: Oxford University Press, 1985).

120   *The result is often a rat race in which all must work until eight o'clock each evening merely to avoid falling behind:* For a formal model incorporating

this interpretation, see George Akerlof, "The Economics of Caste and of the Rat Race and Other Woeful Tales," *Quarterly Journal of Economics,* November 1976, 599–617.

121   *In September 2006, the organizers of Madrid's annual fashion week:* Associated Press, "Spanish Fashion Show Rejects Too-Skinny Models," www.msnbc. msn.com/id/14748549.

122   *Young girls aspire to look like the catwalk models:* Associated Press, "As Models Strut in London, New Call to Ban the Skeletal," *New York Times*, September 17, 2006.

125   *According to the National Highway Traffic Safety Administration:* For a detailed discussion of the decision of whether to require seat belts in school buses, see the National Highway Traffic Safety Administration, "School Bus Crashworthiness Research," http://www-nrd.nhtsa.dot.gov/departments/nrd–11/SchoolBus.html.

125   *school buses have tightly compartmentalized seating with tall, shock-absorbing backrests:* Nick Anderson and David Cho, "Bus Crash Renews Debate on Seat Belts," *Washington Post,* April 19, 2005, B1.

126   *One influential school of economic thought holds that law evolves in ways that promote efficiency:* For an eloquent defense of this premise, see Richard Posner, *Economic Analysis of Law*, 2nd ed. (Boston: Little, Brown, 1977).

127   *But the special interests view is not without explanatory power of its own:* For an early description of this view, see George J. Stigler, "The Theory of Economic Regulation," *Bell Journal of Economics and Management Science,* Spring 1971, 3–21.

127   *Evidence that using a cell phone while driving increases the motorist's likelihood of having an accident:* See S. G. Klauer et al., *The Impact of Driver Inattention on Near-Crash/Crash Risk* (Springfield, VA: National Technical Information Service, 2006). Also available at www-nrd.nhtsa.dot.gov/departments/nrd–13/810594/images/810594.pdf.

128   *more than 110 attempts to ban radar detectors in 33 states have been defeated:* National Conference of State Legislatures, "Radar Detectors, Lasers and Scanners: A Legislative Overview," hwww.ncsl.org/programs/transportation/radar.htm.

129   *Surveys consistently show, for example, that more than 90 percent of all people believe themselves to be above average:* For a fascinating survey of the evidence on overconfidence, see Thomas Gilovich, *How We Know What Isn't So* (New York: Free Press, 1990).

Chapter 7 • Decoding Marketplace Signals

133 *Yet studies of these recommendations show them to be astonishingly one-sided:* Roni Michaely and Kent Womack, "Conflict of Interest and the Credibility of Underwriter Analyst Recommendations," *Review of Financial Studies* 12, no. 4 (1999): 653–686.

133 *more than 99 percent were either strong buy, buy, or hold:* See www.turtle-trader.com/analysts-bias.html.

135 *for a signal between potential adversaries to be credible, it must be costly (or at least difficult) to fake:* John R. Krebs and Richard Dawkins, "Animal Signals: Mind Reading and Manipulation," in J. R. Krebs and N. B. Davies, eds., *Behavioral Ecology: An Evolutionary Approach* (Oxford: Blackwell Scientific, 1984), 282–309.

140 *Given this choice:* R. H. Frank, "How Long Is a Spell of Unemployment?" *Econometrica*, March 1978, 295. By contemporary standards, the excerpt shown is a tame example of formalism in economic models. But to avoid embarrassing a specific professional colleague, I decided to use an excerpt from one of my own papers.

141 *For instance, in an article entitled "The Tactical Strategies":* Maria Lugones, "The Tactical Strategies of the Streetwalker," in *Pilgrimages/Peregrinajes: Theorizing Coalition Against Multiple Oppressions* (Lanham, MD: Rowman & Littlefield, 2003), 207–237.

143 *This asymmetry can have dramatic implications for the pricing of used cars:* For an extended discussion, see George Akerlof, "The Market for 'Lemons': Quality Uncertainty and the Market Mechanism," *Quarterly Journal of Economics* 84, no. 3 (1970): 488–500.

145 *The sophomore slump is an example of what statisticians call regression to the mean:* For a more formal discussion of this phenomenon, see T. D. Cook and D. T. Campbell, *Quasi-Experimentation: Design and Analysis Issues for Field Settings* (Chicago: Rand McNally, 1979), 52ff.

147 *The explanation involves the same statistical phenomenon—regression to the mean—that accounts for the sophomore slump of rookies of the year:* Daniel Kahneman and Amos Tversky, "On the Psychology of Prediction," *Psych Review* 80(1973): 237–251.

147 *a nurturing managerial style is more likely to elicit good performance from employees than a highly critical style:* Robert Cialdini has found that even praise recognized as insincere has positive effects on performance. Robert Cialdini, *Influence: Science and Practice*, 3rd ed. (New York: Harper Collins,

1993). See also Thomas C. Gee, "Students' Responses to Teacher Comments," *Research in the Teaching of English*, Fall 1972, 212–221; Winnifred Taylor and K. C. Hoedt, "The Effect of Praise on the Quantity and Quality of Creative Writing," *Journal of Educational Research*, October 1966, 80–83.

Chapter 8 • The Economic Naturalist Hits the Road

149 *Psychologist Jerome Kagan has argued that many cultural norms are more fruitfully viewed as adaptations:* Jerome Kagan, *The Nature of the Child* (New York: Basic, 1984).

150 *Yet only slightly more than half of the 70 billion aluminum beverage cans:* Container Recycling Institute, "The Aluminum Can's Dirty Little Secret," http://container-recycling.org/mediafold/newsrelease/aluminum/2006–5-AlumDirty.htm.

151 *Yet almost 90 percent of the aluminum beverage cans sold in Brazil are recycled:* Aluminum Association, "Brazil World Record Holder in Aluminum Can Recycling Rate," www.aluminum.org/Template.cfm?Section=Home&template=/ContentManagement/ContentDisplay.cfm&ContentID=6669.

151 *According to Pat Franklin of the Container Recycling Institute:* Pat Franklin, "$600 Million Worth of Used Aluminum Beverage Cans Landfilled in 1996," http://container-recycling.org/mediafold/newsrelease/aluminum/1997–4alum.htm.

155 *In September 2006, it was 4.6 percent in the United States but 8.7 percent in Germany:* "OECD Standardized Unemployment Rates," www.oecd.org/dataoecd/46/33/37668128.pdf.

156 *The short answer is that the United States imposes a tariff of more than 100 percent on imported sugar:* Thomas Pugel, "How Sweet It Is (or Isn't)," in *International Economics*, 13th ed. (New York: McGraw-Hill, 2006), p. 202.

156 *For example, the sugar tariff was estimated to increase the annual profits of one large producer in Florida by some $65 million:* Thomas Pugel, "How Sweet It Is (or Isn't)," in *International Economics*, 13th ed. (New York: McGraw-Hill, 2006), p. 202.

158 *Because of Singapore's high population density, the country's government has taken several aggressive steps to curb pollution and congestion:* For a summary of the Singapore government's levies on private cars, see ExPat Singapore, "Owning a Vehicle," www.expatsingapore.com/once/cost.shtml.

161 *On average, Japanese couples spend more than twice as much to celebrate their weddings as American couples do:* Miki Tanikawa, "Japanese Weddings: Long and Lavish (Boss Is Invited)," *New York Times*, February 26, 1995, http://query.nytimes.com/gst/fullpage.html?res=990CE7D6143FF935A15 751C0A963958260.

Chapter 9 • Psychology Meets Economics

163 *Much of the pioneering work in behavioral economics was done by two Israeli psychologists, Daniel Kahneman and the late Amos Tversky:* Daniel Kahneman, Paul Slovic, and Amos Tversky, *Judgment Under Uncertainty: Heuristics and Biases* (New York: Cambridge University Press, 1982); Thomas Gilovich, Dale Griffin, and Daniel Kahneman, eds., *Heuristics and Biases: The Psychology of Intuitive Judgment* (New York: Cambridge University Press, 2002); and Richard Thaler, *The Winner's Curse* (Princeton, NJ: Princeton University Press, 1994).

163 *they asked a sample of undergraduate students to estimate the percentage of African nations that are members of the United Nations:* Amos Tversky and Daniel Kahneman, "Judgment Under Uncertainty: Heuristics and Biases," *Science* 185 (1974): 1124–1130.

164 *Cornell University has a suicide rate of 4.3 per 100,000 student-years, which is less than half the national average for university students:* Katharyn Jeffreys, "MIT Suicides Reflect National Trends," *The Tech,* February 18, 2000, http://www-tech.mit.edu/V120/N6/comp6.6n.html.

164 *For example, when people try to estimate the frequency of a given event, they often use the availablility heuristic:* Amos Tversky and Daniel Kahneman, "Judgment Under Uncertainty: Heuristics and Biases," *Science* 185 (1974): 1124–1130.

165 *As Itamar Simonson and Amos Tversky have shown:* Itamar Simonson and Amos Tversky, "Choice in Context: Tradeoff Contrast and Extremeness Aversion," *Journal of Marketing Research*, August 1992, 281–295.

169 *A more promising explanation is that hotels may be reluctant to antagonize their customers by charging what are perceived to be unfair prices:* Richard Thaler, "Mental Accounting and Consumer Choice," *Marketing Science*, Summer 1985, 199–214.

169   *Contrary to this pattern, however, recent years have seen a large increase in outsourcing of custodial services:* For a discussion of this phenomenon in the higher education industry, see Geoffrey White and Flannery Hauck, eds., *Campus, Inc.: Corporate Power in the Ivory Tower* (New York: Prometheus, 2000).

170   *employees performing a given task earn higher salaries when they work for more prosperous employers:* For a survey of relevant evidence, see Richard Thaler, "Interindustry Wage Differentials," *Journal of Economic Perspecitves*, Spring 1989, 181-193.

171   *Arcnet, a wireless telecommunications company in Holmdel, New Jersey, hoped to slash its recruiting and training costs by offering a "free" BMW sedan:* CNN.com, "Some Employers Shift into High Gear to Keep Good Workers," www.cnn.com/US/9907/01/wage.pressures.

172   *economist Richard Thaler, who observes that the best gifts are often things we're reluctant to buy for ourselves:* Richard Thaler, "Mental Accounting and Consumer Choice," *Marketing Science*, Summer 1985, 199–214.

173   *people's choices are shaped to a considerable extent by a psychological drive to construct and preserve individual and group identity:* George A. Akerlof and Rachel E. Kranton, "Economics and Identity," *Quarterly Journal of Economics*, August 2000, 715–753.

182   *southbound drivers would experience total combined waiting time of twelve minutes and thirty seconds:* If no one followed the first-come, first-served norm, all northbound cars would cross the bridge first. The first crossing would take thirty seconds, but each successive northbound crossing would be completed just ten seconds after the one preceding. So by the time all northbound cars had crossed the bridge, the first car in the southbound would have been waiting for two minutes (30 seconds for the first northbound car to cross, plus an additional 10 seconds for each of the remaining nine cars). The waiting time for the second southbound driver would be ten seconds less (since he arrived 10 seconds after the first southbound driver), and each successive southbound driver's wait would be ten seconds less than that of the driver just ahead. So the total waiting time for the ten southbound drivers would be twelve minutes and thirty seconds.

182   *If you are patient enough to add up the relevant waiting times, you will see that total waiting time would be eighty minutes:* The first northbound car would cross, then the first southbound car, then the second northbound

car, then the second southbound car, and so on. In that case, the time spent waiting to enter the bridge would be just thirty seconds for the first southbound car (90 seconds less than before). So the norm produces a good outcome for the first southbound driver. The second northbound car would spend fifty seconds waiting to enter the bridge (the 20 seconds remaining in the first northbound car's crossing plus the 30 seconds required for the first southbound car's crossing). The second southbound car would wait one minute and twenty seconds to enter the bridge (since it arrived 10 seconds after the first cars, it had to wait the 20 seconds remaining in the first northbound car's crossing, then 30 seconds each for the first southbound and second northbound cars to cross). For drivers behaving in accordance with the first-come, first-served norm, the resulting arrival, bridge entrance, and waiting time for each car in each caravan is summarized in the table below.

1. Arrival Time (Minutes:Seconds)

	1	2	3	4	5	6	7	8	9	10
Northbound cars	0:00	0:10	0:20	0:30	0:40	0:50	0:60	0:70	0:80	0:90
Southbound cars	0:00+	0:10	0:20	0:30	0:40	0:50	0:60	0:70	0:80	0:90

2. Bridge Entrance Time

	1	2	3	4	5	6	7	8	9	10
Northbound cars	0:00	1:00	2:00	3:00	4:00	5:00	6:00	7:00	8:00	9:00
Southbound cars	0:30+	1:30	2:30	3:30	4:30	5:30	6:30	7:30	8:30	9:30

3. Waiting Time (= Entrance Time - Arrival Time)

	1	2	3	4	5	6	7	8	9	10	Total
Northbound cars	0:00	0:50	1:40	2:30	3:20	4:10	5:00	5:50	6:40	7:30	37:30
Southbound cars	0:30+	1:20	2:10	3:00	3:50	4:40	5:30	6:20	7:10	8:00	42:30

80:00

Chapter 10 • The Informal Market for Personal Relationships

184 *Women generally confess to being attracted to men who are financially success-ful:* D. M. Buss and M. Barnes, "Preferences in Human Mate Selection," *Journal of Personality and Social Psychology* 50 (1986): 559–570.

184 *Although men never used to mention earning power when asked to list what they find attractive in a woman, they have begun to do so in recent U.S. surveys:* Deborah Siegel, "The New Trophy Wife," *Psychology Today*, January-February 2004, www.psychologytoday.com/articles/index.php?term=pto-20040107-000008&page=1; "What Men Want from Marriage," *Ladies' Home Journal's Special Report*, June 2003, www.meredith.com/NewsReleases/Mgz/LHJ/lhj0603stateofunion.htm.

185 *In the United States, the average age at first marriage in 1960 was 22.8 years for men and 20.3 years for women. By 2004 these ages had increased to 27.4 and 25.8:* Data are from the U.S. Census Bureau's *Current Population Survey*, March Annual Social and Economic Supplements, 2004 and earlier.

185 *The average age at first marriage in Australia in 2001 was 28.7 for men and 26.9 for women, up from 23.4 for men and 21.1 for women in 1970:* See Australian Bureau of Statistics, *Yearbook Australia,* 2004, www.abs.gov.au/Ausstats/abs@.nsf/Lookup/62F9022555D5DE7ACA256DEA00053A15.

187 *Between 2000 and 2003 the average age at first marriage in largely rural West Virginia was 25.9 years for men and 23.9 years for women:* See U.S. Census Bureau. For women: www.census.gov/population/www/socdemo/fertility/slideshow/ACS-MF/TextOnly/slide11.html. For men: www.census.gov/population/www/socdemo/fertility/slideshow/ACS-MF/TextOnly/slide12.html.

190 *According to one early study:* Paul H. Jacobson, "Differentials in Divorce by Duration of Marriage and Size of Family," *American Sociological Review,* April 1950, 239.

190 *a plausible hypothesis is suggested by:* See "Uniformed Services Former Spouses' Protection Act Bulletin Fact Sheet," http://www.dod.mil/dfas/militarypay/garnishment/fsfact.html.

191 *Evolutionary psychologists Satoshi Kanazawa and Jody Kovar, for example, offer persuasive evidence for the following four propositions:* S. Kanazawa and J. Kovar, "Why Beautiful People Are More Intelligent," *Intelligence* 32 (2004): 227–243.

191 *It is said that gentlemen prefer blondes, and in many Western countries survey evidence confirms this:* See, for example, S. Feinman and G. W. Gill, "Sex Differences in Physical Attractiveness Preferences," *Journal of Social Psychology* 105 (1978): 43–52.

195 *The important point is that even though such emotional commitments foreclose potentially valuable opportunities, they also confer important benefits:* For an extended discussion of this point, see R. H. Frank, *Passions Within Reason: The Strategic Role of the Emotions* (New York: Norton, 1988), chap. 10.

196 *Evidence suggests that people who consciously approach those relationships in scorekeeping terms are less satisfied with their marriages:* B. Murstein, M. Cerreto, and M. MacDonald, "A Theory and Investigation of the Effect of Exchange Orientation on Marriage and Friendship," *Journal of Marriage and the Family* 39 (1977): 155–162.

Index